STONE COUNTRY

Published by:

Stone Country Press Ltd,
61 Sinclair Drive,
Glasgow,
G42 9PU,
Scotland

ISBN 095487790X

Printed by: Fratelli Spada, Italy

www.stonecountry.co.uk

STONE COUNTRY

Bouldering in Scotland

Written and edited by John Watson

Photography edited by Tim Morozzo

Bob Ewen on 'Watercolour Challenge' - Trossachs

Ben Pritchard on 'The Shield', Dumbarton Rock.

CONTENTS

WHAT IS BOULDERING?

Bouldering is the simplest and purest form of climbing. There are no ropes, no clanking harness-skirt of metal gear, no ice-axes, no pitons, no-one on the telly modestly deferring to talk about near-death experiences… the most you require is a stone at least as big as yourself and a pair of rock-shoes, maybe a bag of chalk to keep the fingers squeaky-dry. You may have driven past a hitcher with a customised mattress on his back, like some colourful giant beetle. You may even come across a group of this species with toothbrushes taped to telescopic broom-handles, obsessed with cleaning and brushing a high hand-hold on an insignificant-looking boulder, surrounded by apparently less attractive crags and mountain routes. What is the point of this, you might ask? Surely there are bigger, more attractive climbs? But that is the nature of the game - it is a climbing obsession with purity, not size. Bouldering is impressive in that it can erase the presence of great cliffs and mountains, focusing the mind down to the child-like simplicity of the climbing act.

Bouldering began as a sub-species of climbing in France, in the great Alpine age of the late nineteenth century. In the mystical forests of Fontainebleau, a train-ride from Paris, Alpinists found a maze of jumbled sand-stone boulders, shaped like mutant beasts, worn into pitiful shapes by the wind and rain. They scrambled on them, then linked together particular short climbs to make a 'circuit' and bouldering was born. Of course, their objective was technique and fitness for higher Alpine climbs, but slowly, over the decades, some individuals saw this short climbing as an end in itself, with 'problematic' moves as hard as any on the big climbs - suddenly they were in their own realm.

The Americans were the next to evolve bouldering and in the mid to late twentieth century, the futuristic vision of John Gill - a bouldering mathematician with a gymnast's power – lifted the activity of bouldering into the pure activity it has now become: the hunt for physically demanding and perplexing short climbs. John Gill's legacy is that you could do nothing else but boulder and still be called a climbing legend.

Back in Fontainebleau, they persevered with this new conception and reduced their climbing addiction to a few athletic moves on an obscure boulder in a whispering birch forest. Soon, there were legends of 'boulder problems' in the forest that were humanly impossible to the casual observer. Nowadays in 'Font', as it is fondly known, there are bouldering activists who boggle the mind with their levitational skills. But it is just an illusion: it is all hard work, repetition and technique.

Now bouldering is a world-wide phenomenon, whose activists feel a sense of community and indeed separateness from the high jinks of mountaineering. That is not to say the mountaineer cannot be a boulderer, or vice-versa, in fact both activities inform each other quite naturally. However, you might say the boulderer is a kind of exiled climber, obsessed with both the minimum and maximum demands of climbing in the same breath. Boulderers, unlike traditional climbers maybe, toy with the idea of blankness rather than size; they explore the boundaries of simple 'climbability'. No-one will ever climb hold-less, featureless vertical walls, but what features are enough? What holds can the body conceive to use? Bouldering is all about exploring the least a rock can offer and what physicality is deemed enough to climb it. And a boulderer demands a problem be done well, so as to reflect the balance between the extreme elements of power and grace - it is best when it looks easy, when there is no redundant effort, nor lack of adequate technique – when there is always just enough.

And what is a boulder? To those who don't climb, a boulder is a blunted, round thing of encroachment and blankness – an obstacle to vision and emotion. Once you climb, the boulder is born – you have pulled out its life. It takes form; it becomes mischievous and throws you off balance, even though it is just a big lump of gravity. You stand looking at it, hands on hips, for hours, chalking up, wondering how the rock got so beautiful and strong and you so weak. But at least the stone now no longer exhibits pure inertia, but has lines of movement and energy, like nerves on an anatomy drawing. By climbing on it you light up its nerve-lines and having climbed its problems, you leave it, for a brief geological moment, switched on like a lamp.

Chris Graham bouldering into the light on the Loch Lomond boulders.

Leaderfoot Viaduct

Wolfcrag Quarry

"...a grade is just
graffiti, like scratching
your name on the
school desk..."

PAINTING NUMBERS ON STONE

There was originally nothing: no numbers for boulders; no natural mathematics for great stones. But boulderers, like chalky maths professors, scrawled their numbers all over the blank zero that is stone. We called these numbers grades and they referred to the difficulty of ascending a boulder, or a line of ascent upon it.

There are now grading systems all over the world, some more popular, or more historic, than others. Most systems break down when trying to delineate movement too closely, but still these systems are followed religiously and obsessively. The reason? The boulderer seeks the validation of a particular grading system to bench-mark his or her prowess. There are many systems in the world: Fontainebleau grades, Vermin grades, Peak grades, British Technical; Australian... the list goes on. One thing they have in common is an apparent mutual exclusivity, with no-one agreeing what 'Font 6a' really is: in British terms, it could be 5c, or it could be 6b: a certain amount of fuzzy thinking is required. Naturally this leads to massive arguments and debates; you can hear them in pubs before closing time: verbal hieroglyphs bubbling from mouths, numbers swarming all over the day's stone.

The grades of the boulder problems mentioned in this book utilise the Vermin grading system which simply goes from V0 to (currently) V15. It is a simple system of exponential difficulty, created by the great American boulderer John 'Vermin' Sherman. Like all grading systems, however, it is the realm of argument, change and subtlety - one person's V5 is another person's V8. Even John Sherman abandoned his own system in time and now just goes bouldering. But at the very least, it gives an indication of difficulty, and by working through the multifarious stones in this book, you will come to find a grade you prefer - one that you, personally, will set as your nemesis, or maybe just the boundary where your strength limitations give way to the need for self-belief.

One thing is sure: you will want to put a number to anything you have climbed successfully, it is hard to resist, but a grade is just graffiti, like scratching your name on the school desk. We are all guilty of this, we all need grades, but ultimately you can either climb the rock, or you can't, and you spend most of the time in between, where there are no grades... where there is simple, numberless absorption.

Lynne Malcolm cruising 'Toto', Dumbarton Rock.

The Thirlstane cave

THE SOLWAY TIDES

We begin our tour in the southwest - on the Solway coast, whose tides come in quick - small hustling armies of waves, attacking the sandstone and greywacke of the northern shores.

Dug in on these shores east of Southerness is an outcropping sandstone boulder with an eroded hole right through it, like a cannon wound through the belly. This is the 'Thirlstane', a 'mill stone' in Lowland Scots. It echoes the 'thirlage man' who, like the boulderer, is bound to grind his grain at the one mill. It lies on the shelly shores of the Solway and attracts dogs and walkers into its smooth-walled cavern where they may come across a boulderer, furiously tending a damp-bleeding hold with chalk-ball, one eye on the tide racing in across the sands, ready to spoil another tired assault on a hard problem. The bouldering has been created on the arched walls of the cave and has generally smoothed crimps and slopers to contend with, the feet often popping off into aidless air, the shoulders swelling like jib sails to take the strain.

The problems are elegant despite their piracy of strength: new classics such as 'Jihad' requiring precise timing and positioning to gain the final holds; or the desperate 'Chinese Democracy' traverse - a product of the dedicated stone-pulling of Paul Savage. There are plenty of reasonable problems and solos and a weekend can quite happily drift away here, as you gather firewood when the tide fills the cave, or sleep in the sun waiting for it to turn, mustering your forces, re-deploying, attending to strategy.

Looming over the shorelines is the swollen heathered dome of Criffel. Crags such as Clifton have birthed some hard boulder problems on the sloping granite lips of its boulder scree, with the scattering of boulders on Criffel itself gives a wealth of short granite bouldering, as hard or as easy as your imagination dictates. Further west along the Solway the geology changes from the tan sandstones and higher, more recent granites to a hardened greeny black sandstone called Greywacke, formed by underwater slippages of muddy sandstone from ancient Silurian earthquakes and metamorphosed into a fine-grained rock.

At Garheugh Point some of this rock has calved into boulders and this was explored by Dave Redpath, excited by a rumour of wave-worn boulders, in weekend raids during the summer of 2001. And so these old boulders and outcrops were given meaning and form and names – some of the boulder problems expressing a sense of new discovery and affirmation of why we move on rock. 'Life is Beautiful' is the perfect bouldering conundrum on the 'Split' Boulder. Many other fine problems have been created on the outcrops and around the classic lines, proving that a sense of exploration and enlightened eyes can pluck out the unseen climbing that still lies in 'un-conceived' rock.

When the tide goes out from our mainland mentality of 'routes' - when we see revealed a new geology of climbing - worthiness is found in this micro-exploration. Along the endlessly fractal coastline of Scotland, bouldering activists are also performing an act of creation in itself, deliberately willing the act of pure climbing from the macro view of mountaineering, and for that we should be grateful and attentive.

'Jihad', the Thirlstane.

THE THIRLSTANE

On the A710 west from Dumfries, the Solway Coast road passes south through New Abbey, under the big mound of Criffel and through the village of Kirkbean, shortly after which is a left turn seawards, colourfully signposted to the resort of Southerness. Take the first left shortly after a farm and carry on round a sharp bend. Take a right turn at the 'Arbigland' signs down to Powillmont farm, and on to the parking by the shore. From here it is a short walk eastwards along the shingle beach to the dramatic Thirlstane itself. Bring a dry rag or two, lots of chalk and a good picnic. If the tide is in, you could spend your time solo-ing the easier routes, or adding more decoration to the shell trees.

RIGHT WALL

The Corner – on the right of the bay just inside the cave proper. This obvious long problem takes a high line up into the roof of the cave, squeezing out right of the chock-stone. *The Niche* - slightly further in on the right is a darkening pod, which is tricky to get into and grunts up and left onto the steep wall to improving territory up a crack. *Tied Up and Swallowed* - further into the cave, after a blank section, is a chin-level sloping shelf where several problems start or end their journey: this direct mantel somehow gains the sloping shelf, using a crimp and powerful contortionism to gain an easier finishing break. *Jihad* - a bona-fide peach of a problem, monkeying left from the sloping shelf to an obvious pocket, from where good positioning and targeting might gain the slopey break. If you latch the throw, traverse happily left to escape. The more direct finish of *Nitro* is also good, and maybe a grade harder. *Bad Sneakers* - this is a direct crossover sequence on the high pockets left of Jihad, just as the cave opens out to the sea. *Chinese Democracy* - when the tide is well out you might want to try your luck with this absorbing and sick-hard sequence from a sit-start at the sea entrance, to finish up Tied Up and Swallowed (if you can stomach it after the traverse). This is one of the 'Sav's' gnarliest creations. The traverse has few foot-holds and long moves and stays as low as possible.

LEFT WALL

Route One - the left wall's problems start at this imaginatively named problem. It lies just inside the cave at a groove which is climbed from slots, requiring a dose of power at the start. *Shrinking Violet* - just to the right again is a dark evil blankness. This problem takes the obvious challenge of the wall, direct from a vertical slot – take a torch and have faith in the thought that it has been done! *Endrina* - the roof inside the cave, which muscles backwards on slopers to gain the lip, slapping along left to better holds and finishing up the tight groove right of the chockstone. *Eazy Roof* - takes the next 'roof', left of a flake crack, from a standing start on good holds to a break and rock-over. *The Bad Seed* - this starts under the seaward roof, at a curious inverted heart: taking a crimp and pocket, boom up and right to unseen slots, then pull up to the break. *Hardcore Superstar* - fondly recorded by Paul Savage as 'awesome'. From pockets by the sea entrance, it traverses in footless over the shingle, drops under the roofs where feet can thankfully be used again, then spans out across an impasse to hopefully finish up the blank wall groove.

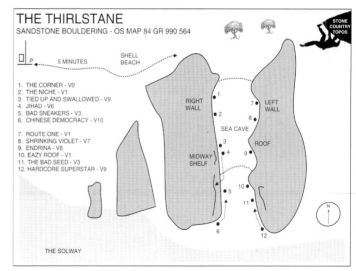

THE THIRLSTANE
SANDSTONE BOULDERING - OS MAP 84 GR 990 564

P 5 MINUTES — SHELL BEACH

1. THE CORNER - V0
2. THE NICHE - V1
3. TIED UP AND SWALLOWED - V9
4. JIHAD - V6
5. BAD SNEAKERS - V3
6. CHINESE DEMOCRACY - V10
7. ROUTE ONE - V1
8. SHRINKING VIOLET - V7
9. ENDRINA - V8
10. EAZY ROOF - V1
11. THE BAD SEED - V3
12. HARDCORE SUPERSTAR - V9

RIGHT WALL — LEFT WALL — SEA CAVE — ROOF — MIDWAY SHELF

STONE COUNTRY TOPOS

THE SOLWAY

N

CLIFTON

A jumble of granite boulders underneath the southwest-facing crag provides some hard test-pieces from Paul Savage. Clifton crag can be approached via the A710, then take a right turn signposted 'Southwick Cemetery' about a mile west of Caulkerbush, then follow the road up to where the crag appears on the right. Park carefully at the cemetery and strike directly up over the fields to the crag then skirt north along the boulder jumble. Three main boulders lie under the crag and provide some hard problems. The landings are often bad and require good spotters and a mat or two to protect the ankles.

Knife Party is a safe problem however! Traverse the slopey lip of the gate boulder from the far right to the top left – best done in cold conditions! *Trauma Arête* lies on the perched boulder up and right. The central face has a bottomless arête and is climbed from beneath to give a hard and worrying testpiece. Further right lies a boulder leaning over the grass. *Zillion Dollar Sadist* sit-starts on sloping ledges and gains the slopey lip, traverses this and finishes up the short arête. There are plenty of other amenable problems on the crags and in the boulder jumble.

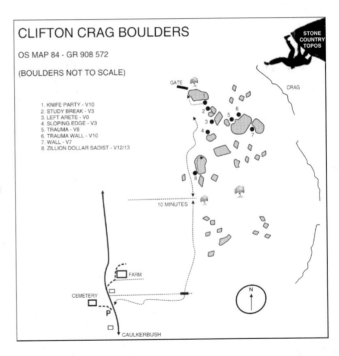

CLIFTON CRAG BOULDERS

OS MAP 84 - GR 908 572

(BOULDERS NOT TO SCALE)

1. KNIFE PARTY - V10
2. STUDY BREAK - V3
3. LEFT ARETE - V0
4. SLOPING EDGE - V3
5. TRAUMA - V8
6. TRAUMA WALL - V10
7. WALL - V7
8. ZILLION DOLLAR SADIST - V12/13

STONE COUNTRY TOPOS

GATE

CRAG

10 MINUTES

FARM

CEMETERY

P

N

CAULKERBUSH

Top to bottom:

1. 'ZDS' boulder
2. Clifton boulder jumble
3. Paul Savage's 'Knife Party'

CRIFFEL BOULDERS
GRANITE

OS MAP 84 (BOULDERS NOT TO SCALE)

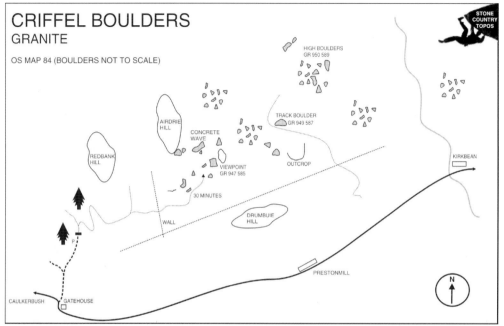

STONE COUNTRY TOPOS

HIGH BOULDERS
GR 950 589

AIRDRIE HILL

CONCRETE WAVE

REDBANK HILL

VIEWPOINT
GR 947 585

30 MINUTES

TRACK BOULDER
GR 949 587

OUTCROP

KIRKBEAN

WALL

DRUMBUIE HILL

P

PRESTONMILL

N

CAULKERBUSH   GATEHOUSE

CRIFFEL BOULDERS

On the flanks of Criffel lies a long and impressive boulder jumble. When you stumble upon it, you may think it one of the best-kept secrets of Scottish bouldering – miles and miles of boulders eventually thinning out as they climb the heathered granite dome of Criffel itself. It is a great venue in early summer before the bracken obscures the boulders, with its fine outlook over the sun-glittering sands of the Solway estuary.

They are best approached from the forestry tracks just east of Caulkerbush. Turn into the forest at a gatehouse and veer right up a track to a locked gate. Take the triple switchback forestry track up right for fifteen minutes until the forestry clears and the granite boulders begin to appear ahead. Veer off on a smaller track and cross the old stone dyke and make your way up to the Viewpoint boulder, which is obvious when you gain a bit of height. From here a veritable smorgasbord of boulders becomes visible. Try not to drool too much and aim for the bigger boulders, as many shrink disappointingly on approach. It is a venue to boulder at will and problems have not been described due to their complexity and/or eliminate nature. Take a small mat and wire brush and create your own problems, there's plenty for everyone.

Left to right:

1. 'Concrete Wave' boulder
2. Tricky granite slabs!
3. Viewpoint boulder

GARHEUGH POINT
GREYWHACKE BOULDERS

(OS MAP 82 GR 267 501)

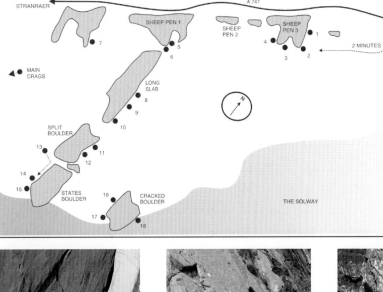

STRANRAER

A 747

B7005

WIGTOWN

2 MINUTES

MAIN CRAGS

SHEEP PEN 1

SHEEP PEN 2

SHEEP PEN 3

LONG SLAB

SPLIT BOULDER

STATES BOULDER

CRACKED BOULDER

THE SOLWAY

1. AFTERLIFE - V7
2. MR. PRICKLES - V3
3. PRINCESS - V0
4. SUCK MY WOOLIE - V6

5. SNOWHITE - V6
6. STRETCH ARMSTRONG - V7
7. SCREAMER'S SLAB - V1
8. NUCLEAR PUPPY - V3
9. THE RAMP - V0
10. DUMBY BOYS - V2

11. LIFE IS BEAUTIFUL - V4
12. BOWFINGER - V7

13. MIKE'S TRAVERSE - V6
14. ALTERED STATES - V7
15. CHANGING STATES - V4

16. THE MANTLE - V0
17. SHADOW DANCER - V4
18. BARNDOOR CRACK - V1

Clockwise;

1. Garheugh Point
2. 'States Traverse'
3. 'Changing States'
4. 'Snowhite'
5. 'Life is Beautiful' footwork

16

GARHEUGH POINT BOULDERING

Further west along the Solway on the A75 road to Stranraer, the A747 can be gained from just before Glenluce, 15 miles west of Newton Stewart. Follow this for 10k to a layby on the right at the top of a hill before the B7005 to Wigtown. The boulders and crags are a short scramble down to the sea. Or, carry on past the junction and park by the shore and walk along - the first problems are on the Slab Wall, which has a sheep pen behind it. Long baggies are useful for some of the problems, as is a good lifting technique for shifting sea-transported boulders. Approaching from the east parking spot, the first big slab appears and has some great highball problems.

Mr. Prickles - This climbs the slab-side of the tall left arête from sharp sidepulls. A thriller! *Afterlife* - Further right, this levitates up the apparently blank centre of the slab. Highball. *Suck My Woolie* - On the other side of the slab, by a sheep-pen, this excellent problem snaps up undercuts at the bulging nose, from a sit-down start, then climbs into the easier hanging groove of the next problem. *Princess* - This takes the highball cracked groove, gained from ledges just right of the above.

Further along the shore are the main boulders and the long slab. The sheep pen beside the long slab has two good strenuous problems: *Snowhite* - This sit-starts from the crimps on the boss under the arête, slaps up right for the lip and pulls awkwardly over onto the slab. *Stretch Armstrong* - A more direct solution to the last problem, this crosses through from the same boss to the arête and climbs it direct. *Nuclear Puppy* - This climbs the short crack to the right of and gaining the midway ramp, on the Long Slab. *Dumby Boys* - This good problem starts near the slab's left edge, by the brambles, launches from a jug, then tiptoes up right and back breathalysingly left to finish. *Screamer's Slab* - Behind the Long Slab is another tapered slab, which can be climbed direct to the apex on small holds.

Life Is Beautiful - The delightfully scooped crackline. By far the most classic line here, taking the challenge of the crack from a sitting start, technically positioning hands and feet so the reach can be made to the right ledge to finish up the easy hanging slab. The crux is an early press move on the right arm on small foot-smears to match the finger-slot. *Bowfinger* - The centre of the wall is climbed direct via a seam to gain a high diagonal crack.

The States Boulder is the sea-washed lower boulder and has its best lines on the west face. *Changing States* - This climbs the seaward arête: from a crimp behind the right flake, gain the arête, then use slopers and cunning to gain the jug. *Altered States* - A sit-down start gaining the last problem from the powerful undercuts. *Mike's Traverse* - The line of sloping ledges traveling right has good lip-monkeying, but needs a mat or two to protect the ankle-munching pebbles.

The Cracked Boulder is the most tidal boulder, with its obvious problem of: *The Mantle* - The crack can be traversed along from right or left, to mantle carefully into the central groove. *Shadow Dancer* - This takes the sit-start at the sloping seaward corner and gains the sloping ledge on the right, then regains the arête directly. *Barndoor Crack* - On the east side, above a filled-in rock-pool, this testing crack problem is hard to get into and hard to press out to better holds, good balance required.

'Life Is Beautiful' - Garheugh Point.

17

The Stronachlachlar Dyno.

BOULDER VERSUS MOUNTAIN

"I have spent many a happy hour debating the nature of climbing, mainly in pubs, or cars, to the point of folding my arms and not buying another round, or squealing on the brakes and opening the passenger door. In relation to bouldering, there are those who take exception to the notion that it is 'the poetry of mountaineering', as is often quoted. They feel it is in some way a bastardization of climbing; that it is too rigid in its strictures; that it is an incomplete experience – it is climbing without all the normal expectations of the climber: remoteness, adventure, risk, responsibility, time, situation, height, comradeship... but maybe this is more a case of not looking out of the corner of their eyes. The point of bouldering can easily be missed, because the object seems so minimal. For the boulderer, these same elements do exist, albeit in a smaller theatre. You do all these 'mountaineering' things when you throw your rock boots in a sack with a toothbrush and a bag of chalk. For example, there is nothing riskier than finding a remote boulder and worrying the integrity of your ankles with a belly-flop over the unclean brow of a vegetated top-out. There is the adventure of discovery, of finding that *El Dorado* boulder somewhere in a deep and mossy forest. I have heard of boulderers who buy helicopter videos, or search the internet for aerial photography, just to discover isolated erratics with that tell-tale shadow denoting steepness. Others have hacked the Ordnance Survey codes for 'boulders' and run searches for these alone, then printed out the maps. Why so much fuss over something so small? Because the code of climbing is adventure, exploration, self-expression, freedom, and these are found in boulders as readily as mountain peaks.

Not all rock insists on being climbed in one manner; often there is as much latitude in a boulder as a mountain: there are always harder or more elegant solutions to climbing it. In fact, with all the repetition, new techniques are discovered, often through simple comradeship under the stone, and a whole range of emotions is unleashed when the 'line' you stick your faith to finally pays off. Many boulder problems take months to complete, eclipsing even the most dedicated alpinist in terms of hours: both are chasing the same arbitrary goal of the 'summit'. Similarly, it is the whole thing that counts, not just the summit, and when it's over for the mountaineer, the same things are remembered by the boulderer: those hours sheltering from the rain, waiting for the alchemy of conditions; the weakness; the doubts; the digging deep; the obsession; the pain; the sudden evening light that stops you in your tracks. So anyone who comes at me with the argument that bouldering does not exhibit the finest qualities of mountaineering, the passenger door is open..."

Johnny Morozzo on 'Terror Direct', Craigmore.

STONE HEADS

"Just north of Glasgow's claustrophobic industry, and set in a mossy old forest littered with quiet boulders, lies an escape for the day. A place of abandoned care, forgotten duty and total absorption: Craigmore. Pinnacles and boulders sit propped up against the crag like fallen idols or unfinished heads from a Glaswegian version of Easter Island. The rock is quartzy, compact basalt with a tendency to toothbrush up to dimpled slopers and fierce crimps. On a cool sunny evening in spring or autumn, powering through the problems, the trees whispering in a light breeze, it leaves the city boulderer transported. The classic problems here all require balance in the body and steel in the fingers, as well as wisdom in choosing the right time to go: a cool breezy morning in summer or spring after a dry spell is magical, but especially during a dry autumn spell. On a badly chosen day, a hot still evening in summer for example, fingers pop off, feet skitter and the midges can follow you high enough to where they know you can't let go."

Pete Murray on 'Jamie's Overhang'.

CRAIGMORE
BASALT BOULDERING

(OS MAP 64 - GR 528 798)

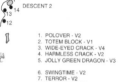

1. POLOVER - V2
2. TOTEM BLOCK - V1
3. WIDE-EYED CRACK - V4
4. HARMLESS CRACK - V2
5. JOLLY GREEN DRAGON - V3

6. SWINGTIME - V2
7. TERROR - V2
8. TERROR DIRECT - V4
9. LAYBACK CRACK TRAVERSE - V2
10. SAMSON - V4

11. THE BLADE - V1
12. TARANTULA GROOVE - V1
13. LEECH WALL - V3
14. BLACK BEAUTY - V0

15. PINNACLE WALL - V0
16. SILK PURSE - V1
17. SHORT PINNACLE - V0
18. RED SLAB TRAVERSE - V3
19. ANDY'S WALL - V4

20. THE WIZARD - V5 (SS. V8)
21. SUZY Q. - V0
22. VICTORY V - V2
23. TWO TREE WALL - V0

24. TERMINAL ARETE - V3
25. JAMIE'S OVERHANG - V4
26. SUNSHINE ARETE - V0

STONE COUNTRY TOPOS

Clockwise:

1. 'Layback Crack Traverse'
2. 'Wide-eyed Crack'
3. 'The Wizard' top-out
4. 'Terror Arête'
5. 'The Wizard sit-start'

CRAIGMORE BOULDERING

From Glasgow the A809 aims for Drymen and Loch Lomond. After the biker-haven of the Carbeth Inn, take the first right along the B821 link-road to Blanefield. After the green hut community of the forest, the crag is on the left, hidden in trees by the fields, just before the West Highland Way. East facing, it is best on a dry morning in spring or autumn. The best of the bouldering can be completed as a Fontainebleau-like circuit, providing a good work-out on varying styles of problem. The Southern section is predominantly bouldering on the main crag buttresses, while the Northern section gives dispersed boulders and walls all the way to the end.

Polover – Takes the right hand crack of the first wee buttress. It is a good introduction to the treacherous nature of sloping footholds at Craigmore. Finish by stepping right onto the arête and down-climb.

Totem - Stuck in the corner like a discarded statue is a totemic boulder with an undercut midway crack: pull on to this block in the centre and gain the sloping jugs at the top; back strain can be eased by clever footwork.

Wide-Eyed - A classic! Just right of Totem is a crinkle-cut crack in the wall. Lunge to the break in the centre and lock-off up to a foot-popping stretch for reluctant holds, while balancing tension and composure. Finish by down-climbing right or solo-ing the easy but heart-fluttering headwall.

Harmless - The crack just to the right. Gain the lock in the crack, where a different sequence is required depending on which hand you use.

Jolly Green Dragon - Round the corner is a blunt arête right of a holly corner. This excellent eliminate problem sit-starts at a V-hold down and right, booms up to the finger-slopers, then snatches all the way up to a sloping ledge. Finish right.

Terror - Past the classic corners of the crag, a large nosed boulder appears just before the Layback Crack on Craigmore Wall. Overbearingly named, it is more a subtle flying arête. The original line climbs the left side to finally insist on unsettling reaches from a strained position, whereas the superb *Terror Direct* reaches cunningly up from the big slot on the overhanging wall to gain the high left crimp which allows the faint right crack to be won.

Layback Crack Traverse - The crag to the right can be traversed at foot level from a sit-start at the left arête to finish at the corner left of Samson.

Swingtime - A fun problem and well-hidden! Find the cave in the woods just below the Terror boulder. From the cave's jammed blocks, throw in a big foot-jam and cross through to a hold on the sloping lip, then cut loose and swing left to hook the lip. Finish by dropping down left and rocking out on the downward lip.

Samson - Past the Layback Crack main wall, a short blank wall is encountered left of a stepping-stone boulder: This old test-piece undercuts powerfully left to a slopey barn-door manoeuvre to finish at better holds in a groove.

The Blade - Climb this cleaned face to rock out left at the top and climb *a cheval* to the top.

Tarantula – After The Blade, the crag turns up-hill after the big groove of Autobahn. The first scooped recess round the corner has a hanging groove which can be climbed on good holds to finish up the wall. Highball.

Leech Direct - The second recess has a fine horizontally cracked wall over a ramp. Climb to the break, employing faith and good lock-offs, or you are trampolined into the ferns. *Leech Arête* is the superb balancy blunt arête to the left, pulling round onto the wall to gain the original problem.

Black Beauty - The wee uphill block by the descent gives a good crack problem.

Pinnacle Wall - Climbs the first tall pinnacle under a tree – it is a highball but steady climb to the top.

Silk Purse - Just to the right is a wee buttress. Sit-start at its right arête and climb this to rock round right onto the north wall, with a crux cross-over to sloping lips up and right.

Red Slab - Traverse this coloured wall from the left edge past a difficult blunt undercut to a wee crack and better holds.

Andy's Problem - Just right again, a wee bulging wall provides a difficult sloper problem. From a sit-start, slap right to a lip sloper, gain another, then snatch up and left to a better hold and rock-up to finish.

The Wizard - This is a challenging and crimpy arête, which can be climbed from standing, or from the wee cave as *The Wizard Sit-Start* at V8. It leads to an ethical decision at half-height as to whether this is a step-off boulder problem or a route!

Victory V - The roofed buttress to the right of The Wizard gives an eliminate sit-start leftwards to trend up a hanging arête – no bridging.

Two Tree Wall - From the last problem, traverse right under the roof and swing out onto the right wall and finish direct. Highball.

Jamie's Overhang – At the end of the crag, under the protective pine, is the leaning block which hides the best problem here. The roof has various levels of eliminate difficulty. The original line hunkers down in the hole, snaps from the break up to a good left hand-hold, and then swings in a controlled fashion to the far right sloper where good finishing gains a sharp crimp and a tricky rockover. *Surprise Attack* aims straight to a sloper in the middle of the lip and rocks over. This hard eliminate is the most powerful problem here.

Terminal Arête - The long, steep-side of the propped block can be climbed by using both arêtes and bear-hugging up the wall on smears. More technical than it looks.

Sunshine Arête – Just under the pine, balance up and sit under the big tree to ponder the boulder vastness of the Highlands...

23

Exploring a Small Space

It's an old problem. This nagging voice in my head:

"Left foot up to the hold, then stand on it, up with the left hand to the big pocket!"

It won't shut up; I'm tired of hearing it. And besides, there's a crystal at the base of the pocket that I've twisted my fingers into; it's ripped a big hole in my index finger. They say bouldering in the cold guarantees best results, but not when the crux is still damp and slippery and my finger feels like someone's been hitting it with a hammer for half an hour. Time to move on.

A week later, and Colin's counselling me: "Your arse is too far out. You need to drop your left foot." So, I'm up there again, and suddenly my left foot is lower down. It shouldn't be able to stick there; the afternoon sun is gleaming off that smooth section of the sloping crack below me. A better climber would call it a toe jam, and I'm sure it'll slip, but now I'm pulling on the thin flake, and I realise I can pull up my right foot.

"I've never been here before," says the voice. Then it falls silent.

I'm not conscious of my feet pushing on anything to get here, or my arms pulling, yet the fingers of my left hand are sunk up to the palm in the narrow break of the finishing jug. The Austrian boulderer Klem Loskot says when you're climbing at your limit, pulling the hardest moves you can, it's as if a space opens up under you; you don't feel your weight any longer. It feels like you can do anything.

David Cairns writes of rock acting on us like the moon upon the sea. The salt-and-pepper basalt of Craigmore is the closest lowland Scotland has to gritstone. Mini-towers, slopers, dry, crystally friction, and all of it within an hour of Glasgow on a bike.

Almost abandoned by most serious climbers, the solitude of the place pulls me back time and again, like a tide. Hardly a surprise: the basalt that makes these walls and cracks is the same stuff as the surface of the moon and the ocean floor. Like the ocean, the rock's still alive. I might be obsessed by the tiniest contours of this open, grey crack, and the dark spots on the wall that mark the good smear for my right foot. But above me, the last few metres below the top are slippery with the damp lichen that's reclaiming much of the crag, taking the surface back to nature, despite the occasional intrusion of chalk, stealth rubber or wire brushes.

For the first time, I'm looking at a gossamer curtain of frost on the surface of the moss and heather at the top of "Wide Eyed". It's held so much attention and ambition for me, and for so long, that I don't really want to come down. But these moments of silence are valuable because they are so short.

When I started climbing, a little over ten years ago, Ben Moon wrote: "6c just isn't that hard any more, and 6b is approaching a rest". It'll never be that for me and it's no big deal in the overall scheme, but when I started, this level was unthinkable, so it's hard to believe I'm here.

The memories come: on the top deck of the bus heading in for the night shift. Boots and chalk bag stuffed into the pockets of my coat. Like a clumsy chef I have one finger taped up, but this cut didn't come from a kitchen. I'm learning that rock injures, as much as it welcomes our attention.

Moss, rock, leaves - the smell lingers like the scent of a lover's sex on my fingertips - as evocative to me now as the incense that lingered in church after funerals as an altar boy. But I discarded religion at the same time as my school uniform. And now I'm smelling a new kind of life on my hands. The movement, the new friends, new music, new places; so vivid and fresh, it feels like living in a film.

There are casualties, of course: broken ankles, broken teeth, one elbow squeaks like a broken hinge; in the morning, my right hand feels like it's wrapped inside the pressure sleeve the doctor uses to check my blood pressure; and when I'm hard on myself, one broken relationship with the mother of my kids. But then, many small charges blew us apart. Climbing was only one of the detonators.

What gets anyone into a place like this? When I started out, to solo something even well within what I could climb was to stare into a well of horror and fear. Yet, I'm up at the top of this micro-route, no rope, harness or wires, pulling on tiny flakes, fingers slowly slipping out of this cross between a slopey crack and a triangular pocket, the movement of one foot marking the difference between just another boulder problem and succeeding on the hardest problem I've ever pulled. I realise I'm not scared.

Where does the fear go? Does it just fall silent like that voice in your head? Terror transforms to confidence. Or, maybe the first guru of bouldering, John Gill understood it best of all. Bouldering has a mathematical logic. You only have to work out the calculus of the movement. Fill your brain with those sums, and there's no space for anything else.

So, ticking "Wide Eyed" was never just a question of linking hard moves - climbing is always about linking imagination and desire. Power and technique are only the means to an end until you can also imagine your own success. Life can be like a film. Staring at the screen of this laptop, the small scar on my index finger takes me back to Craigmore.

It's an old problem: pulling through the crux will silence the chattering voice, but pulling into that silent space only opens up more small spaces to explore...

"Shall we move on?"

Pete Murray 2004

Gary Vincent on 'King Kong'

THE BLACK FONTAINEBLEAU

Dumbarton has long had a litter of dolerite boulders suckling on the great mother-rock, well before humans stuck a castle and a wee blue and white flag on top of it. It bubbled out of the Clyde Plateau lavas 340 million years ago, through a generous crack in the earth's crust. Vikings besieged it and left. William Wallace fumed in prison here. A young Mary Queen of Scots looked out fearfully from the ramparts. During World War Two, it was even bombed by the Germans, who believed it to harbour stupendous guns. The boulders remain, quietly unmoved, scrambled on by kids so they can throw bottles from the mini-summits and paint graffiti as high as they dare. 'Dumby', as it is affectionately known, is a tawdry place, the boulders stained by impromptu driftwood fires and splashed with paint and angry young names and slogans. Broken glass crunches underfoot and in winter the boulders turn green and drip under the great open bible of the main face. But to climbers it is the gypsy queen of Scottish bouldering. The weird Picasso cubism of the fractured rock gives it a complexity and class of movement totally unique to itself, revealed only through repeated and often perplexing physical scrutiny. After a few visits in springtime, the graffiti dissolves before your eyes; the broken glass a glinting path leading to your favourite problems. The sounds you hear are the boulderer's constant friction between success and failure: squeaking chalky cracks, roars, great slaps, howls of exasperation, barks of encouragement...

This is where Scottish bouldering was conceived, as early climbers 'practised' on the boulders with one eye on the main face lines, getting used to the slope and treachery of high holds, learning what could be stood on and what couldn't, training the head to stay composed and focused at chaos-inducing heights. All the oft-quoted names of Scottish climbing have cut their teeth, amongst other things, on these boulders: Neil MacNiven, Brian Shields, 'Cubby' Cuthbertson, Gary Latter, Andy Gallagher, Malcolm Smith, Dave MacLeod... behind these names are legions of talented climbers and visitors who have climbed at this 'Black Fontainebleau', who have either run away in disgust and fearful confusion, or come back for the blood count of bagging the big or the hard. Problems like 'Gorilla', 'Toto', 'Mugsy' and 'Pongo' do not relent easily, and the modern test-pieces like 'The Shield', 'Pongo Direct', 'Sabotage', 'Firestarter', 'King Kong' and 'Shadow' require the dedication of the hardened alpinist and the bloody-minded fitness regime of a marathon runner. Like a Black Hole, Dumby will suck in the light from all other bouldering in Scotland; it is the indisputable heart of its philosophy.

The best desecent off the BNI boulder, Dumbarton Rock.

Dave MacLeod on his long-term roof project.

HAPPINESS IN SLAVERY

'The early December light faded as I shuffled about on my mat, brushing, feeling and then pulling on for all of three seconds before pretending to slap for the lip with one foot already back on the ground. 3pm drifted into 3.30, into 4. "Got to get this move sussed". The black, dingy cave seemed grimmer than ever as the day slowly passed into night. I couldn't even wander around the boulders between attempts. A curtain of drips drained off the lip of the cave, forming a neat moat of puddles guarding the entrance to the home of my 'project'. "Ah well, at least its still climbing outdoors" I told myself.

My dreary winter afternoons in the cave were just about the loneliest place all my years of climbing has taken me to, yet all around was human activity. Across the River Leven, a JCB shifted rocks back and forth, repairing a sea defence. Nearby, a fierce-looking chap strolled by, clutching a large air rifle. He stopped beside a thorn bush, picked up an old can of Tennent's (not hard to find among the boulders) and propped it on a branch. After walking a sporting distance from it, he turned and began shooting at it (at a trajectory uncomfortably close to me). In the distance, trains rolled by, car horns honked, and school football teams shouted "Tae me, tae me!"

Why was this more lonely than, say, a freezing belay, eight pitches up on Ben Nevis as the daylight slipped away and my partner's rope paid out inch by inch? I had become so drawn into the moves of this project and the intense concentration required that the rest of the world drifted further and further into the background. Confined to my cave by the rain and locked into my attempts by a combination of frustration and curiosity, I concentrated and pulled harder. The language of the experience was pure climbing; crimps, slopers, lunges, hip shifts, timing, precision, aggression; pure movement. There was nothing in the way. No ropes or harnesses, other climbers, weather or danger - just cold black basalt, and me.

This intensity was exactly what I was after. A more gentle experience could be had from any of climbing's other disciplines. I was not missing such experience. On the Dumbarton boulders there were no excuses, no distractions; just movements, and that's the way I liked it. Why could I not experience this in a nice warm climbing wall or cellar board? Why did it need to be on a dismal winter evening at the rock? The answer is that the projects are real, the lines have been there since the ice ages and I have imagined climbing them since I first visited the place, ten years ago.

The December cold made conditions realistic for attempts on a line at my physical limit, the absence of other people eliminated distractions, and the constant rain prevented me from straying off to easier lines, shying away from the massive effort needed even to work the moves. I felt a special connection with this line, the horizontal black roof under 'Gorilla'. It was always that joke line that we made fun of as young climbers, pretending to power between its tiny holds that would be impossible to hang by even the best climbers around at the time.

Actually, it would have remained a joke line if it hadn't been for my inadvertent involvement in the creation of a more realistic sequence of holds. In 2002 I had climbed everything that I could climb on the boulders and took a long break from visiting the Rock. I only returned briefly when I realised a link-up of three existing problems would provide a good challenge to keep me occupied for a bit. This line, 'King Kong', climbed the Gorilla arête in its entirety at a tough 8a. On one attempt something peculiar happened. While slapping into the starting holds on 'Silverback' I kicked the roof as usual with my left foot to help twist my body in the desired direction. As I did so I heard a big thud. A fairly gentle tap with my foot (by rock breaking standards anyway) had dislodged a seemingly solid block about the size of an electric toaster. This dropped to the ground leaving behind an elegant flat layaway, which looked like it had been designed to be used as a hold.

In a flash, the huge roof had gone from 'impressive but impossible' to faintly realistic, in a Font 8b+ sort of way! From a sitting start with toe hooks it was just possible to reach the hold. Then, after working the feet up it would be possible to slap, at maximum span to the lip of the cave. Beyond that, a small undercut and another slap might gain a flat jug at the base of an equally blank overhanging wall. I reasoned that if you could get that far, the rest of the problem would unravel. I knew I could climb it someday, but not the following week or even the following few years! I certainly didn't intend to be drawn into battle now.

It all went wrong in October 2003. With a confident spring in my step after succeeding on Sabotage earlier in the year (another line on the boulders which had seemed impressive but impossible just a short time before), I let myself get attached to it. After a couple of days slaving away in the cave trying to work out a sequence, I looked back on previous Dumbarton obsessions to get a bit of inspiration and perspective.

One thing was for sure; every project I'd ever tried I'd stuck with to the bitter end. Happily, the end had always been success. I felt quite proud of this, but realised that a few of those successes had cost me dearly.

'Consolidated' nearly had me thrown out of school at 16. I remember explaining to the school board director that I wasn't wasting my life and that I could still pass my exams. Thankfully, he was a climber and understood my motivation, (so I escaped expulsion by a whisker) but he still predicted my academic failure. A four day bout of anorexia saw me through that pumpy hand change and back in the classroom, but it was too late to pass and I paid through the nose with night classes two years later.

'The Shield' had little chance against my bottomless motivation, but my body gave in instead. I thought tendonitis happened to old climbers. I remember the final sickening acceptance as I packed away my rock shoes that I wouldn't be seeing a crag again for a long time. I also remember the 5th of November 1997; pulling onto the rock again for the first time after 5 months of frustrating physiotherapy: one of the best days of my life.

'Pongo Sit Start' tested my patience across 4 years. It looked so climbable, yet that flake always remained just out of reach. Then, after all those days of frustration and having been beaten to the first ascent, I finally found the sequence that worked for me, it was easy!

'It seemed that success on the problems at the Rock was especially elusive, often hanging in the balance of seemingly small and unpredictable factors.'

It seemed that success on the problems at the Rock was especially elusive, often hanging in the balance of seemingly small and unpredictable factors. This was both a depressing and empowering conclusion. Given that the Gorilla cave line was clearly a huge jump in difficulty above anything else that had been climbed; I could be facing decades rather than just months of frustration ahead. What a thought! On the other hand, if I could free myself from the impatient need to see the line as a complete entity which must be climbed from bottom to top before I could reap any satisfaction, I could happily sidestep any frustration. In this way, could I just enjoy every inch of progress, no matter how small, with the complete link remaining the ultimate but distant goal?

The first challenge was to climb the finishing wall from a standing start (an inspiring line in its own right). With an overhead heel hook between my hands I could move out across the wall on tiny edges. Then, two left hand slaps might gain a good diagonal edge below the top. I sensed success and started to really fight. Once again I was taught my lesson; never try to beat a Dumbarton problem with pure brawn. I screamed and hit the good edge, but both hands exploded off. With my heel still locked in the good hold, I flipped upside down and slammed head first into the ground. After a month of trying, I felt calmer and more respectful and suddenly I could get to the diagonal edge every try! All that was left was a scary leap to the finishing jug, out of sight beyond an overlap. For ten tries I leapt but missed, leaving big chalk hand-prints just below the jug, somersaulting through the 'jaggies' and broken bottles below. On the last try of the evening, with strength failing but aggression coming under control, I leapt and held the top – 'Firestarter' was born, 8a in its own right and a big hurdle overcome.

All the time I was playing on the roof underneath, and could do all but one move; to slap the lip from the new layaway. I got more excited with each session as I could touch the lip, then almost hold the swing. After about 20 days in total, I finally found a better way to grasp a crucial intermediate hold and held the lip next try! "Bloody hell, this could really happen!" I jumped straight back on to try linking the move into the finishing wall. Then, pulling harder than ever on the intermediate, I exploded off the rock and winded myself landing flat on my back. The hold had ripped off the wall and bounced off my head to add injury to insult.

I stomped home in disgust. The project had just moved the goal posts. Was I suddenly years rather than weeks away from linking it? I also wondered if it actually mattered. With so many projects in the past I'd gone through the same process of doubting only to have done them a few days or weeks later. Success or failure was only a self-imposed judgement. In fact, the feeling of failure I'd attached to this winter-long endeavour seemed entirely false. All that came through was the memory of sheer effort and surprising progress.

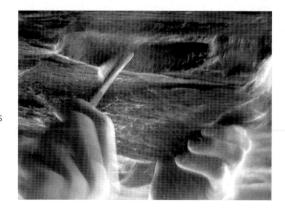

After a few days I was already missing the moves and felt ready to return. As ever it was pissing down. I crawled through the hole in Safeway's fence and strolled across the puddles and tangled metal of the waste ground, leaving the rest of the world behind once more for another afternoon as a happy slave.'

Dave MacLeod - 2004

Mal Smith on BNI Direct.

DUMBARTON ROCK
DOLERITE BOULDERS

(OS MAP 64 GR 400 745)

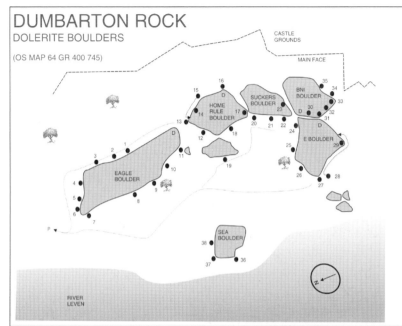

CASTLE GROUNDS

MAIN FACE

HOME RULE BOULDER

SUCKERS BOULDER

BNI BOULDER

EAGLE BOULDER

E BOULDER

SEA BOULDER

RIVER LEVEN

N

1. CENTRE DIRECT · V0
2. PULL-OVER · V0
3. ZIG-ZAG · V1
4. SHADOW · V7
5. HIGH-FLYER · V6
6. FIRE-STARTER · V11
7. GORILLA · V4 (SS. V7)
8. SUPINATOR · V3
9. 2HB · V3
10. OCEANS · V8
11. BLUE MEANIE · V2

12. HOME RULE · V3
13. MESTIZO · V3
14. MUGSY · V5
15. MUGSY TRAVERSE · V8
16. THE BEAST · V0
17. THE WHIP · V2
18. ROUTE ROYALE · V3
19. FRIAR'S MANTLE · V1

20. TOTO · V3 (SS. V6)
21. THE SHIELD · V8
22. THE RAILINGS · V3
23. VOLPONE CRACK · V0

24. SLAP HAPPY · V6
25. PONGO · V5 (DIRECT V11)
26. SORCERER'S SLAB · V0
27. NEMESIS · V1
28. CONSOLIDATED · V8
29. HARD CHAEDDAR · V2
30. DEO GRATIS · V1
31. IMPOSTOR ARETE · V0
32. B.N.I. DIRECT · V2
33. SABOTAGE · V13
34. GOOD NICKS · V3 (DIR. V8)
35. PENDULUM · V1

36. EREWHON · V1
37. STEPTOE · V0
38. WHITE WALL · V2

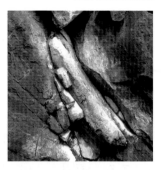

Clockwise:

1. Holds on 'Pongo'
2. 'The Shield'
3. Industria
4. 'Good Nicks Direct'
5. 'Erewhon'

33

"The perennial Dumbie experience is going through that sort of blocky, black, shattered stuff that looks like it should have holds but you're just 'Rolfing' around trying to find a wee edge somewhere......very sequency, very hard to onsight. 'Blue Meanie' is a good example of that style…"

Graham Foster

'Blue Meanie', Dumbarton Rock.

EAGLE BOULDER

The first boulder you arrive at under Dumbarton castle, this boulder invites you into a ritual of physical heroism - a huge rock with a symbolic Lion Rampant on its seaward slab, the overhanging faces challenge you to highball and impending lines. Eagle Boulder, more than any other stone, might leave you feeling like you've just walked unscathed from a car-crash...

Gorilla - The seaward face has a string of classic problems, the most obvious challenge being the flying prow of rock pointing towards Ben Lomond. From two permanently chalked crimps on the roof, a haul or jump gains the subtly notched layaway: both techniques require precision, so there is no shortcut. The ape-like swing to the nose can be cunningly controlled before the final rock-over onto the slab, which will leave you clear-eyed and ripped with a feeling of sudden initiation. The sit-start travelling left at the crimps through crux slopers to climb the prow direct, is *King Kong V11*.

Supinator - A highball crack problem which demands a careful rockover finish; as the name suggests, carelessness can leave you on your back in the brambles.

2HB - Behind the sycamore tree, this delightful mental and physical entanglement initiates the first-timer into the precision required to enjoy Dumbarton bouldering. Climb up right and aim for a two-finger undercut, then boost for ledges – they are good.

Oceans - Takes the scooped orange wall just right of the tree. From an undercut and a right hand press crux, smear desperately left and gain edges to a scary finish up and left.

Blue Meanie - Just up the path, this shattered roof forces you to lean leftwards over a jagged plinth, but there are good holds to top out on. Start at good holds and aim for a layaway, then reach hopefully left for the jugs.

Centre Direct - Climb the centre of the slab direct – it blanks out a bit at the top. Highball.

Zig-Zag - The roof on the right of the slab. After having been teased through the roof on big holds, the sudden conundrum of stepping left at overlaps might gain easier ground.

Tam's Route - Just round the corner is the black and brooding overhang facing the entrance path. The most left-hand groove can be climbed on flat holds, leading to a thin and often green top-out.

Shadow- Just to the right is an impressively scary overhanging black groove, which sees few ascents, requiring mainly a rush of blood to the head. A steep start on poor holds leads to a direct finish up the groove.

High Flyer - Takes off from a flat hold on the right of the roof and gains the hanging ramp to finish. An awkward start from the plinth that needs a good spotter and bags of commitment to make the initial jump.

HOME RULE BOULDER

This boulder has until recently held the lion's share of test-pieces at Dumby.

Physical Graffiti - Gary Latter's challenge up the face looking over the River Leven, climbing straight above the graffiti and on up into the un-painted, emotional blank canvas of loneliness.

Home Rule - A less scary but classic sequence, pinching and rocking up to the handrail, with the best finish traversing left to finish up the thin moves on the classic arête of Mestizo.

Mugsy - The secret to the wall above the cave was discovered by Scottish all-rounder Dave 'Cubby' Cuthbertson: 'simply' a matter of combining strength and technique with a dynamic approach. From the flat lip holds, heel-hook, crimp and slap up on slopers to a good jug in the middle of the wall, finishing carefully left or right. Can be climbed by a jumping start. The traverse along the lip to finish up Mestizo is an excellent V8.

Mestizo - The arête is climbed from a pinch and side-pull: a wee jump allows the left foot to be placed, then an undercut allows the spike higher right to be gained. A thin sequence rocks up the highball groove to finish. Downclimb the 'ridge' facing the crag.

The Whip - The Clyde-side prow, with its hanging groove over sloping grass, has one of the best highball problems at Dumby. Climb the groove right of the starting arête beside Sucker's Boulder. It stops you in a high position with an essential but terrifying commitment to more delicate climbing up the rib on the left.

Joe Newman on 'Mugsy'.

Chris Boutell showing us how it's done on 'Toto'.

SUCKER'S BOULDER

Squeezed out by its bigger brothers and flanked by two caves, this boulder still manages to give us some classic problems.

Toto - You are likely to find a conspiracy of grounded boulderers contemplating this 'disappearing' crack. First unravelled by the Scottish pioneer Gary Latter, 'Toto' is a deceptive pull and step into a crack and scoop that leads, eventually, to a jump-off jug up high on the left. When done well by a familiar, it looks like a path. However, on first acquaintance, it is a desperate exercise in all things the boulderer holds dear: technicality, commitment, subtlety and strength. A good V7 sit-start, travelling along the fingery handrail to lurch for the bottom of the original, was worked out by Andy Gallagher in 1996.

The Shield - Malcolm Smith's classic power problem. The obvious eponymous challenge lies to the right of Toto and requires massive pressing strength and sharp reactions to hold the slopers at the top. Use any holds you like on the 'shield', pull on, get your feet high and slap with either or both hands to the lip - it's hard whichever way! A sit-down was added by Dave Redpath at V10.

Totality - The missing link between Toto and The Shield. Travel right once on Toto, on poor holds, and get a toe on the Shield. Then aim up and right and try not to slip off.

Volpone - The hanging slab crack is a good fun problem, with polished footholds. Eliminates on the thinner slab to the left have been climbed.

B.N.I. BOULDER

Despite developing equipment and fitness levels in bouldering over the years, there is always the Bloody Nigh Impossible! This boulder pays respect to that enduring humility - it is a historic Scottish boulder that has seen epochal ascents. It seems to prop up 'Sucker's' boulder and the long but low 'E' boulder, like an elder with its prodigies, and it has stories to tell.

Imposter Arête - In the late 50's and early 60's, Neil MacNiven and Brian Shields crawled up the 'descent' hole and walked up this exposed arête, climbed on its left side, where they got the idea of stepping right onto the orange slab...

B.N.I. - The hanging orange slab. Step right from Imposter and tip-toe right to climb the right side of the slab to an overlap and easier but highball ground.

Deo Gratis - The seaward slab above the descent hole, climbed in the centre to an undercut crux move on a small foot-nick - a heart-fluttering moment to a 'thank-god' hold.

Pendulum - More of a route! Climb to the big jammed block on the ledge, then use hidden holds to swing round onto the arête slab and finish easily.

Good Nicks - In the '70's, Willie Todd cranked out this old peg crack which then aims high and left for a stretchy finish round the right arête of BNI.

B.N.I. Direct - In the '90's, Mal Smith powered straight through the roof onto the slab with *BNI Direct*. Start at the rock plinth and pull up, then try and get your toe on and gain the high crimps on the slab.

Sabotage - More recently, in 2003, the awesome dedication of 'Dumby' Dave MacLeod paid off to give one of Scotland's most physically demanding problems, which takes the challenge of the roof and apparently hold-less nose of the boulder. From a sit-start in the cave, climb the hanging arête to a crux sequence through poor slopers on the nose to gain the slab.

Joe Newman on 'Good Nicks Direct' - V8.

The dynamic approach to Andy Gallagher's classic 'Slap Happy'.

E BOULDER

This - possibly the most communal of all the boulders at Dumby - aptly has our most common letter 'E' to name it. It seems unassuming enough until you try the harder problems or the traverses, then it unleashes its brutality and usually leads you scuttling away, badly beaten, to an easier problem.

Pongo - The obvious roof-crack is a case in point. Endowed with excellent-looking holds, it requires proper hydraulics as you pull on. A dynamic leap for layaways from the poor hand-rail leads to powerful locking manoeuvres and teeth-clenching finger-locks. The 'sit-down' version of *Pongo Direct* requires the utmost of butch approaches and shoulders like tightened Meccano. Originally climbed by Mal Smith, it was a watershed in what was possible in Scotland and is probably the most lusted-after modern problem at Dumby. Gain the first big slot, then the famous shoogling jammed block, where a long throw for the layaways leads to a howlingly hard crux press into the original problem.

Slap Happy - Andy Gallagher had given us an idea of how hard things could get with this now classic campus problem. From a good flat ledge right of the cave, crank through finger edges on the leaning wall, requiring a kind of surprise attack on gravity to gain the holds at the lip. Rock over to finish and punch the air. The crucial foot-hold is becoming more and more polished.

Consolidated - Traversing came of age on this boulder when the awkward seaward nose of *Nemesis* suggested you could drop down on slopers to continue up and right on the lowest of sloping holds, chalk-bag trailing the ground, to turn the corner and finish by the cave at whatever finish you had the strength left to try. Andy Gallagher started all this off in 1994 and now the lowest, thinnest finish goes at about V11. The crux sequence round the nose involves dropping down under the green scoop to a triangular hold, where a boost to the easy wee arête proves frustratingly hard after all the effort just gone.

Hard Cheddar - The flying slabby right arête of this boulder is the usual cop-out finish from the crux corner of the Consolidated traverse! Use flanges to lunge up and right to jugs - with little purchase for the feet.

'Bob's Bitch', Sebastopol Boulder, Trossachs.

A BAG OF CHIPPED MARBLES

Mica-Schist is the rock that dominates the Central Highlands. It is a densely scalloped metamorphic rock, squashed by ancient pressures, veined with quartz, sometimes flaky as pie-crust, sometimes granitic and rough as high-grade emery paper. For some it is an acquired taste; providing either finger-splitting crimps or endless slopers, (or both!) but it is a technical rock despite its variable form. One thing it does provide is plenty of boulders: great roofed chunks that have calved from the crags or been plucked out by glaciers and shunted around the quiet glens. They are everywhere and reward attention - every boulderer can claim one as a pet, only it's like keeping an eagle; it flails at you, cuts your skin with its quartz beaks and talon-edged pockets.

There are countless bags of chipped marbles in the Central Highlands: Glen Croe, Ben Ledi, Glen Ogle, Tarken Glen, Glen Massan, Carrick Castle, Inveruglas, Loch Katrine, Loch Lomond, Stronachlachlar, Craig Hulich, Glen Lednock... there are simply too many to mention and it is the message of this book to suggest that bouldering is infinite; its prizes reward the explorative and curious climber - the stone hunter, the climber that puts on the brakes at every crag and forest-glimpsed stone; or the dreaming, optimistic boulderer who climbs high into the hidden corries and glens, imagining fields and fields of beetling boulders... quite often you will not be disappointed. The hours will pass by like time-delay clouds as you dab and brush and pull and slap... the Central Highlands require only good legs and a love of solitude. Here is a selection of the most recently developed schist boulders discovered so far, though it is by no means exhaustive - the rule of this land is adventure.

Fighting schist.

41

LOCH SLOY
MICA SCHIST BOULDERS

(BOULDERS NOT TO SCALE)

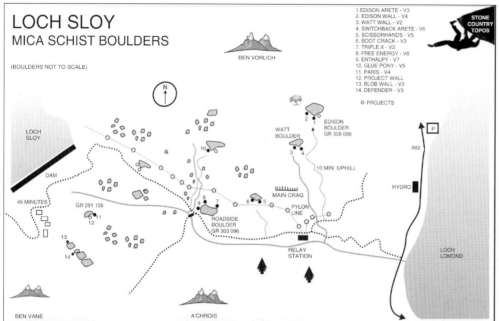

1. EDISON ARETE - V3
2. EDISON WALL - V4
3. WATT WALL - V2
4. SWITCHBACK ARETE - V6
5. SCISSORHANDS - V5
6. BOOT CRACK - V3
7. TRIPLE X - V2
8. FREE ENERGY - V8
9. ENTHALPY - V7
10. GLUE PONY - V5
11. PARIS - V4
12. PROJECT WALL
13. BLOB WALL - V3
14. DEFENDER - V3

○ PROJECTS

STONE COUNTRY TOPOS

BEN VORLICH

N

LOCH SLOY
DAM
45 MINUTES
GR 291 106

WATT BOULDER
EDISON BOULDER
GR 308 096

10 MIN. UPHILL

MAIN CRAG
PYLON LINE

ROADSIDE BOULDER
GR 303 096

RELAY STATION

HYDRO

A82

P

LOCH LOMOND

BEN VANE
A'CHROIS

Clockwise:

1. Dave Redpath on 'Defender'
2. Dave MacLeod on 'The Project'
3. Dave MacLeod on 'Blob Wall'
4. John Watson on 'Watt Wall'
5. MacLeod on 'Free Energy'

42

LOCH SLOY BOULDERING

On the west bank of Loch Lomond, a few miles north of Tarbet on the A82, park at Inveruglas and walk back past the Hydro station and up the private road by Inveruglas Water into the seclusion of Coiregrogain, surrounded by three Munros. At the switchback road by the relay station, either climb up the blunt ridge by a burn to the Watt and Edison boulders on a high alp, or continue along the track into the glen, along which the main boulders lie on the north side of the track: the Roadside boulder is right by the bridge junction. Continuing on up to the dam, over on the south side of the stream, gains the Project boulder and the Blob Wall. The best problems are mostly the blips from the boulder radars of Dave MacLeod, Dave Redpath and John Watson.

'The Edison Boulder' is a high boulder with a tree growing out of its top. The main wall is steep but has good holds. Two excellent problems worth the climb up to them!

Edison Wall - From a sit-down start under the arête, traverse up and left and boom for the high ramp, then monkey right and climb round onto the arête and slab to finish.

Edison Arête - From the same sit down start, go straight up on layaways and pockets, using a crucial pinch on the arête to gain the ramp and same finish.

'The Watt Boulder' lies down and left of the Edison boulder. This has a slabby wall facing south down at the pylon charge of Glen Loin.

Watt Wall - Climbs the central wall and slab direct from the ramp, using sidepulls out left to a high rock up out right to finish direct.

Switchback Arête - A very problematic arête, which forces you out the wrong way! Come in from the right and reach blindly left round the arête for the pocket, then use the blunt arête and a high sidepull on the right wall to crank up insecurely.

The 'Boot Crack Boulder' lies past the main crag by the relay station: there is a wildly overhanging boulder 100m north of the road.

Boot Crack - The cave crack. Take the obvious highball central crack - a traditional struggle.

Scissorhands - This is the sharp challenge of the scooped wall and arête on the right.

The 'Roadside Boulder' is the obvious bulging boulder by the road at the bridge.

Enthalpy - Climbs from a crouching start on edges in the centre of the vertical wall facing the dam: get a good left crimp, then a mono pocket, then slap for the diagonal crack.

Free Energy - Dave MacLeod's answer to the bulging nose to the left of Enthalpy. Sit start at a lefthand pocket, throew high for a pocket on right, then climb directly past slopers and quartz nubbins to an awkward snap for the diagonal crack.

Triple X - A more amenable problem taking the left hand crack on the back wall from a sit-down start.

'High Boulder' lies up the hill by the burn from the Roadside boulder, through some small boulders to a higher boulder with a good overhung face and brushed edges.

Glue Pony - Climbs from the glued left-hand hold and pinch on the arête: set your body right and try to hang the sloping slot, then crank up and left to the lip and exit awkwardly into the groove. The hanging face to the right is horrifically steep and unclimbed as yet.

The 'Blob Boulder' lies down from the dam: follow the road right round and drop down to the obvious tall boulder, or skip over the bog to the boulders.

Blobs - Climbs the obvious featured wall on the red blobs, superb, with good holds to finish!

Defender - The excellent arête on the boulder behind the Blob boulder.

'Paris Boulder' lies downhill from the Blob boulder. The truly steep south wall on this boulder provides a stern project wall.

Project - This problem sit starts at the letterbox hold in the centre and gains a poor undercut, then a pinch and sidepulls higher up. A big move might gain the jugs high and right.

Paris - Takes the good right arête from a sitting start.

GLEN CROE
MICA SCHIST BOULDERS

OS MAP 56 (BOULDERS NOT TO SCALE)

1. THE RAMP - PROJECT
2. PRECIOUS - V9

3. SUPERCRACK - V7
4. THE CUTTING ROOM - V8
5. THE NOSE - V3

6. AXEMAN - V10
7. PROJECT
8. ACE OF SPADES - V7
9. PANACHE - V1

10. CRACKHEAD - V4
11. TURBINAL NOSE - V10

12. OSWALD - V3
13. HAPPY B'DAY MR.PRESIDENT - V9
14. ASSASSIN - V3
15. NUCLEAR BUTTON - V9
16. CAVALCADE - V6
17. TRIGGER FINGER - V6
18. CONSPIRACY - V4
19. BRAINS - V3
20. VIETNAM - V4

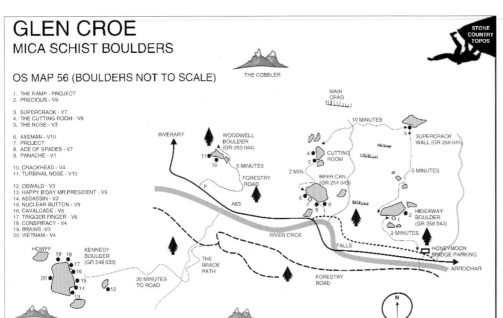

Clockwise:

1. 'Vietnam' - Kennedy Boulder
2. 'Axeman' - Beer Can Boulder
3. 'Turbinal Nose', Woodwell Boulder
4. The Hideaway project
5. 'Cavalcade', Kennedy Boulder

GLEN CROE BOULDERING

As you come into Tarbet from the south, the A82 Loch Lomond road veers left onto the A83 which winds round the sleepy village of Arrochar on the shores of Loch Long, under the devil's horns of the Cobbler. A mile further on, it swings round past Ardgarten campsite into the steep-sided and moody Glen Croe. Many of the boulders in Glen Croe are easily missed, as the Cobbler dominates the attention, but the jungle-like lower slopes below the South Peak, covered in birch scrub and spruce round the tumbling River Croe, hide some giant boulders, wedged into the tufty mountainside like hurriedly buried treasure. Small springs squeeze out from under them and the treasure master has long gone, leaving the boulders in a Gollum-like loneliness, until they were coveted by Mike Tweedley, Dave Redpath and Dave MacLeod amongst others. They can all be approached via the car-park below the falls of the River Croe and there are many boulders to explore and lines to be climbed at all grades.

Thread up left through the stand of trees and mossy boulders by the parking and bog-trot uphill for two minutes. The Hideaway Boulder is the obvious prowed boulder on a kind of mezzanine.

Precious - The impressive prow, climbed by Mike Tweedley in 2003. Crank backwards to a crux pocket-pull through to gain the wall on the right.

About five minutes hike above the Hideaway boulder, and level with the main crag further left, is a steep roofed crag just left of a wee waterfall.

Supercrack - The obvious snaking crack is started from the quartz block on the right and traverses left on hidden holds to crank up to a jammed block, from where it is probably wise to step off and take the points! Climbed by Dave MacLeod, this is again one of the best hard problems in the glen.

The Beer-Can Boulder is the roofed boulder just over the fence behind the 'picnic pool' above the Croe Falls and not far from the road. It can be approached by walking up the track round the craggy nose from the parking spot. The roof provides the best of the problems.

Axeman - The left-hand end of the roof. Crouching from undercuts on the lip, slap up for a sloper above, utilising heels and toes, then find a crimp out left to steady for the final swing of the axe.

Ace of Spades - The crack-line on the right, which can be climbed from a sitting start from pockets, aiming for a good hold high on the left.

Panache - Climbs the right hand slab by the arête, finishing excitingly up and right.

Other good problems lie on the Cutting Room Boulder on a small boggy alp above the Beer Can boulder. *The Cutting Room* - Climbs the razor-edged face of this boulder from a sitting start. *The Nose* - A good problem surmounting the roofed nose to pull over to the hanging slab, climbed from a sitting start.

The Woodwell boulder can be approached from a parking spot just north of the falls. Follow the forestry track round a bend for five minutes or so, to where embedded boulders lie below the track. They have steep roofs facing down the glen.

Turbinal Nose - Another superb MacLeod creation which throws up the hanging arête left of the crack. From a sitting start, slap to a right hand ledge, gain a hold up and left with a long move, then heel-hook to gain another hand-hold. Cross desperately into the high groove to finish.

Crack-Head - The obvious steep crack, from a sitting start - a good natural-looking challenge to any boulderer.

High up above Glen Croe in the dark shadow of the Brack's north face, lies a president of stony time, perched on its grassy knoll, shot through with quartz bullets: the exquisitely named 'Kennedy Boulder'.

It can be seen from the A83, in a corrie bowl just above the last of the forestry, and can be approached from the parking just before the falls of the River Croe. Park by the stand of trees, cross the road and wade the river (or use stepping stones if it's low), then gain the forestry track - follow this rightwards past a junction at the switchbacks and shortly after take the Brack path up by the stream. Once through the forestry, cross the stream and head up right and across to this huge and obvious boulder, set on a small plateau below the main faces. It has two long overhanging roofs and provides steep pulling on pockets and crimps, over grassy landings, so, despite the walk-in, or maybe because of the walk-in, this boulder attracts the aficionado of remote bouldering.

Happy Birthday Mr. President - The steep wall left of Assassin. Sitting from undercuts, bounce up to a good double finger-hold - once matched somehow gain the slopers above.

Assassin - The original classic line on the left of the front face. Sit start under the bulge and take a fine juggy sequence which leads to an awkward mantel out right.

The Nuclear Button - Just to the right: this powerful problem starts from quartz holds directly up to a hollow block, then dyno's wildly for the top – it is slightly easier but good fun from the standing start at V7.

Trigger Finger - On the right of the wee boulder, pull directly through pockets and flakes into the groove to mantel onto the slab.

Cavalcade - Same start as the above, but press out left over the wee boulder to gain a good hold, then boom for the lip...

Conspiracy - The obvious bulge to the right of Trigger Finger. Gain the handrail from a sitting start and then launch for jugs.

Brains - The highball slab facing the glen: committing but not desperate.

Vietnam - On the back face, this excellent problem climbs out from the roof along a handrail, then presses out to a finishing flake.

Bob Ewen on 'Mind Trick', Jawa Boulder.

CLIMBING TOURISM

"If mountaineers are hardened explorers, then I guess boulderers are fanatical tourists. You get this feeling at the Trossachs boulders. These fine stones have just failed to roll off the flanks of Ben Venue and into the south-east basin of Loch Katrine. Situated under the Bealach nam Bo (an old cattle-rustling pass), the outlook is serene and restful, the silence broken only by the tourist spiel on board the 'Waverley' as it steams past. The boulders are unusually compact for mica-schist, granitic in texture, providing moves reminiscent of gritstone. The main sentinel boulders here sit perched invitingly by the path on grassy turf. Approaching them is a delight – they grow in size and apprehend your eye – they have you unclipping the bouldering mat impatiently and you just can't get your shoes on quick enough. The other boulders, scattered around in the trees and by the burns, provide explorative bouldering in sepia-tinted post-card surroundings; the romantic heart of Scottish tourism. Bouldering is just another form of tourism in the long run, but maybe it shares a more explosive approach to the landscape: in Victorian times this was the seat of the great project to douse the throats of Glasgow with fresh mountain water and the area was a hotbed of blasting and pipe-laying, as navvies fought as hard as they worked, giving their bothy shanty names like Sebastopol, after the Crimean War, no doubt due to the rum-fuelled bust-ups amongst this very Gaelic 'bristled ground'. And then they vanished from history, their job done, with a legacy of ingenuity and industrial creativity, as one day the boulderers will vanish, leaving their own small legacy of precision and foul-mouthed genius..."

Dave MacLeod on the 'Jawa Traverse', Trossachs Boulders.

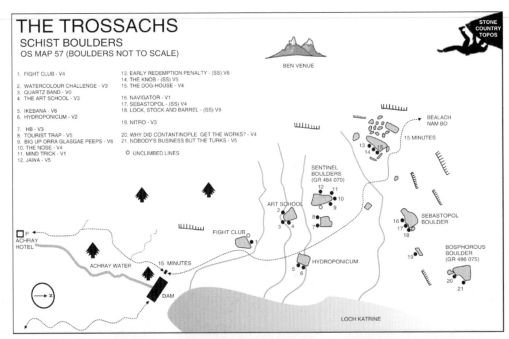

THE TROSSACHS
SCHIST BOULDERS
OS MAP 57 (BOULDERS NOT TO SCALE)

STONE COUNTRY TOPOS

BEN VENUE

1. FIGHT CLUB - V4
2. WATERCOLOUR CHALLENGE - V3
3. QUARTZ BAND - V0
4. THE ART SCHOOL - V3

5. IKEBANA - V8
6. HYDROPONICUM - V2

7. HB - V3
8. TOURIST TRAP - V5
9. BIG UP ORRA GLASGAE PEEPS - V6
10. THE NOSE - V4
11. MIND TRICK - V1
12. JAWA - V5

13. EARLY REDEMPTION PENALTY - (SS) V6
14. THE KNOB - (SS) V5
15. THE DOG-HOUSE - V4

16. NAVIGATOR - V1
17. SEBASTOPOL - (SS) V4
18. LOCK, STOCK AND BARREL - (SS) V9

19. NITRO - V3

20. WHY DID CONTANTINOPLE GET THE WORKS? - V4
21. NOBODY'S BUSINESS BUT THE TURKS - V5

O UNCLIMBED LINES

BEALACH NAM BO

15 MINUTES

SENTINEL BOULDERS (GR 484 070)

ART SCHOOL

SEBASTOPOL BOULDER

BOSPHOROUS BOULDER (GR 486 075)

FIGHT CLUB

P
ACHRAY HOTEL

ACHRAY WATER   15 MINUTES

HYDROPONICUM

DAM

N

LOCH KATRINE

Clockwise:

1. Locking it off on 'Tourist Trap'
2. The foot-popping dyno on 'Jawa'
3. 'Lock, Stock and Barrel', Sebastopol boulder
4. Gritstone-like Trossachs texture
5. 'Ikebana' in The Hydroponicum

TROSSACHS BOULDERING

Over the Duke's Pass from Aberfoyle the A821 drops down to Loch Achray under the dome of Ben A'an. A left turn at the head of the loch leads up to the Achray Hotel. From the back of this a forestry track follows the south bank of the Achray Water along to the dam at the bottom of Loch Katrine in about fifteen minutes. Continuing along the path for another five minutes or so, the first squat boulder appears by the burn's alluvial fan, just after a sluice and holly tree.

Fight Club – Climbs the sloping overhang. It sit starts at a ledge on a patio of stones, takes a good incut, then fights rightwards on slopers to finish up the blunt right nose.

Crossing the burn and then another burn, the path arrives at the two sentinel boulders. The 'Jawa Boulder' is possibly the most distinctive boulder in the Trossachs; it sits on watch above Loch Katrine. It has a fine southern slabby face of compact schist, the centre of which provides the quality conundrum of:

Jawa - A problem that relies on faith in feet and persistence in technique and flexibility. From the finger rail, smear high and either dyno for the top, or gain a left hand sloper and press it out. *The Jawa Traverse* is a left to right traverse and a fine exercise in balance and bizarre foot cross-overs.

Mind Trick - The crimpy wall to the left on this face. Balance on then try and get the right toe higher if you can…

The Nose - A butch problem tackling the sharp snout from the hand ledge on the left.

Big Up Orra Glasgae Peeps - Steve Richardson's 'Dark Side' problem. A desperate mantel off the ledge to a one-finger undercut that is just sufficient to gain a standing position and hence the top.

The heathered boulder under the Jawa boulder is 'The Tourist'. Two overhanging arêtes provide the best interest here:

HB - The right arête from the long hand pocket, which gives a range of choices of holding the arête before the best sequence leads to the vital undercling up and right.

Tourist Trap - The superb left arête. One of the best problems in the Trossachs, it is a desperate search for escape from a sit-down start. With subtlety it can be climbed statically to the pointy sloper. The best finish monkeys left along the lip to finish in the scooped niche.

The 'Art School Boulder' is well hidden, up over the fence in the burn 50m before the sentinel boulders. The two best problems on this are:

The Art School - The committing downstream arête on good rough rock. Sometimes a bit green, but it is a fine sloper problem when dry.

Watercolour Challenge - A delightful problem taking the pocketed wall looking upstream, with a long reach to thankful holds at the top. An aquatic Fontainebleau boulder that somehow found itself in Scotland!

Below the Sentinel boulders in a kind of well is 'The Hydroponicum'. This boulder leans over a stream just before the sentinel boulders and below the path. It has a magnificently steep central problem:

Hydroponicum - Harder if you miss the tricks, start sitting in the fern-garden and pull up on good holds to finish directly up the groove and onto the slab via a good hold. Do it ten times for the training.

Ikebana – A gnarly low traverse which breaks left on poor sidepulls, to gain the wee pockets and then the rail.

The 'Bealach Boulder' is the obvious boulder high up, facing downhill.

Early Redemption Penalty - Starts sitting down just right of the water-pool, cross-handed, right hand in slot, and slaps left, then right into a side-pull. Reach far left for the lip and rock over via a sharp pocket and slot.

The Knob - Starts at the same holds and pulls directly up via slopers and the obvious knob to rock over the lip onto the slab.

The Dog-House - The right-hand arête above the flat block. From a sit-down at the lowest cleaned hold, traverse right, then crank up left to a poor crimp, slap the arête and finish via a mantel or rocking out right.

The 'Sebastopol boulder' lies down the wee glen above a burn.

Navigator - Climbs the groove left of the nose - from a sit-start, contort to gain the lip and get established in the groove. 'Bob's bitch' is the lefthand rockover finish.

Sebastopol - Climbs the groove right of the nose, using technically demanding slopers and hidden holds.

Lock, Stock and Barrel - The sit start to the last problem and quite independent! From under the cave, slap and heel-hook desperately up the blunt arête in the usually vain hope of gaining the good slopers on Sebastopol.

Nitro - Further down the glen is a T-cracked boulder with a shattered-looking belly. This can be undercut to a crimp and dyno to give some fun bicep problems.

Why Did Constantinople Get the Works? On the prow of land overlooking the 'Bosphorous' of Loch Katrine lies a squat boulder propped on another. The cave can be climbed out along the prop boulder and the nose mantelled out right to a diagonal crack to give this lock-off problem.

Nobody's Business but the Turks - Further right a low right to left traverse leads to a hard press move to gain the same crack.

Niall McNair on Left Wall, the Narnain Boulders.

THE NARNAIN BOULDERS
SCHIST BOULDERS

OS MAP 56 GR 272 056

STONE COUNTRY TOPOS

COBBLER

BEN NARNAIN

N

COBBLER PATH

2K UPHILL

P

LOCH LONG

A83

ARROCHAR

8
9
10
11
12
7
5
6
4
3
1
2

1. POCKETS ROOF - V3
2. PROJECT PROW
3. QUARTZ GROOVE - V3
4. LEFT WALL - V3
5. THE PRESS - V2

6. SLAB - V0
7. LEDGE WALL - V0
8. COBBLER WALL - V4 (SS)
9. THE TESSERACT - V6 (SS)
10. THE CRUCIFIX - V3
11. OCCAM'S RAZOR - V5
12. TWO HOT HONIES - V4

THE NARNAIN BOULDERS

These are the remote and high boulders in the corrie below the Cobbler - a wayfaring marker for those approaching the big climbs, or a shelter from inclement January storms. In their own right they are bouldering gems, for the rock is hardened by the exposed situation and it took the explorative fingers of Niall McNair to stop and discover the moves that had lain dormant their ever since John Cunningham and the Creag Dhu club 'practised' climbing on them. There are many good, easier natural lines, but the best of the dedicated problems are the work of two remarkable characters in Scottish climbing separated by five decades: John Cunningham and Niall McNair. The classic problems are:

The Crucifix - The south arête on the Cobbler-facing wall of the top boulder. It is a superb exercise in balance and technique. First climbed by Cunningham in the early fifities, it is probably Scotland's 'first' boulder problem.

Cobbler Wall - To the far left of the Crucifix, this is a clever solution to a puzzling blankness. From a quartz pinch and low right undercut, position yourself carefully to reach a high left two-finger crimp, then find another undercut to gain the pockets and the top (Pic 1).

The Tesseract - The crimpy groove just to the left of the Crucifix arête, climbing up and left through crimps into the Cobbler Wall's pockets (Pic 2).

Occam's Razor - Round the corner, the impressive rippled west wall has this excellent exercise in pain! It climbs the black weep to the right of the Crucifix arête, needing steel in the fingers and grit in the soul (Pic 3).

Two Hot Honies - The central wall is also excellent: climb to a good rail, where worrying reaches gain the top.

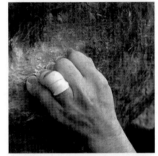

Clockwise from left:
1. John Watson on 'The Bottler'
2. Mike Tweedley on 'The Pit'
3. The crux 'Talon' crimp
4. Mike Tweedley on 'Popeye'

Veering Off the Way.

Though dispersed along a few miles on the West Highland Way, along the pleasant east banks of Loch Lomond National Park, these boulders provide an enjoyable day's adventure and scope for endless bouldering in the densely forested hill-sides where wild goats roam and provide lessons in sure-footedness in the boulder fields. They are best visited in summer when the loch-level is low, after heavy rain the best boulders are swamped. They can be accessed by walking north from Inversnaid, itself accessed from Aberfoyle by a single-track road which somehow accommodates tourist coaches and requires diligent driving. Once on the banks of Loch Lomond, walk north. After ten minutes a dry wall is passed giving the good *Perma-dry Traverse*, climbed from the crack right to left to finish up under the tree.

Five minutes further on, the cluster of man-eating boulders at Rob-Roy's cave is found. The cave is more of a pit itself, but the boulders have some great problems, the best of which lie on the obvious block of 'The Bottle' which lies propped up against other boulders. Many projects remain here, but a few mats and good spotters are useful . The wee cave by the path, under the crag itself, has a fine pocket project coming out to the lip from its dark belly – beware the hibernating bees in autumn!

The Bottler - sit-start at a hole and crank up through quartz holds to the quartz seam, then press and smear out left to a hold in the niche, from where it is wise to step off. *Pit Eliminate* - started from low down in the cave left of The Bottler, this has a crimp-press crux gaining better holds in the light. A few mats and good spotters are useful .

Just before the next bridge, the 'Goat Stone' sits by the track. Its north face has a low lipped overhang. *Goatee* - the right arête can be climbed by snapping left to good holds and finishing up the hanging groove. *Goat-Boy* - the sitting start to the bulge on the left. Lock a right foot down in the low pocket and slap desperately up to quartz edges, where it is frustratingly difficult to get your left toe on to gain the finishing press moves to the right arête.

After the bridge, the gravel beaches appear and the first large boulder on the shore (with the holly tree on it) gives: *Holly's Traverse* – this hooks and boosts left along the full length of the ledges over the gravel to a lovely sequence over the lip to finish up the mossy hanging arête. The *Water-Side Traverse* is also enjoyable.

A little further on, there are boulders at the more open ground of the Pollochro shielings, offering some good problems. *Talon* climbs the scooped wall on the most eastern boulder. Crimp from a sit-start on the left to a fierce finish into the groove on the right. *Pollochro Wall* - the excellent wall facing the loch. Despite a mossy appearance the climbing is good. Step technically up the slabby wall left of the easy groove and gain jugs at the top.

Fifteen fiurther along the Way, the Gate Boulders are reached, opposite Island - I - Vow. The 'Spinach' boulder has a tremendous project roof over fine gravel. *Spinach* - the far-right of the roof can be climbed from a sit-start at an undercut pocket and slopey ledge. Trend left on edges and pinches to rock-up right to jugs. *Pop-Eye* - the north side groove, often over water! This gives superb pocket-pulling... from a sit-start in the V-groove roof by the water, gain the left-hand pocket, then pull hard to Kung-Fu the small mono pocket up right, gain another pocket and boost right to jugs on the arête. *Ug-Ug* - the north wall arête, climbed to the wee tree via a quartz pocket, with a crux sloper move at the top.

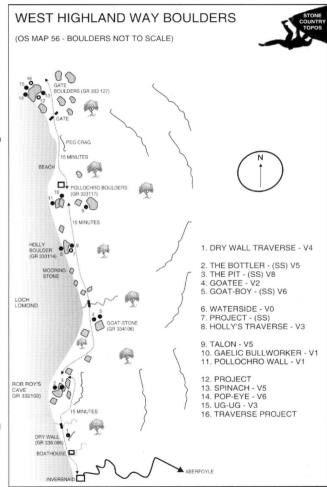

WEST HIGHLAND WAY BOULDERS

(OS MAP 56 - BOULDERS NOT TO SCALE)

1. DRY WALL TRAVERSE - V4

2. THE BOTTLER - (SS) V5
3. THE PIT - (SS) V8
4. GOATEE - V2
5. GOAT-BOY - (SS) V6

6. WATERSIDE - V0
7. PROJECT - (SS)
8. HOLLY'S TRAVERSE - V3

9. TALON - V5
10. GAELIC BULLWORKER - V1
11. POLLOCHRO WALL - V1

12. PROJECT
13. SPINACH - V5
14. POP-EYE - V6
15. UG-UG - V3
16. TRAVERSE PROJECT

BEN LEDI
MICA SCHIST BOULDERS

(OS MAP 57 · BOULDERS NOT TO SCALE)

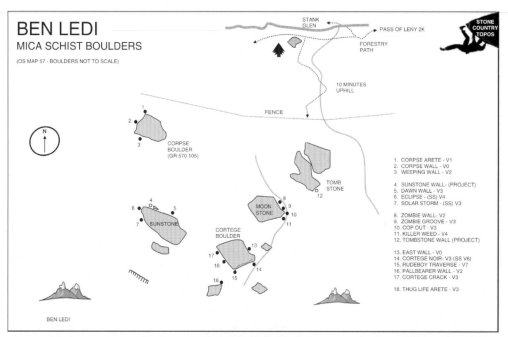

STANK GLEN
PASS OF LENY 2K
FORESTRY PATH
10 MINUTES UPHILL
FENCE

N

CORPSE BOULDER
(GR 570 105)

TOMB STONE

MOON STONE

SUNSTONE

CORTEGE BOULDER

BEN LEDI

1. CORPSE ARETE - V1
2. CORPSE WALL - V0
3. WEEPING WALL - V2

4. SUNSTONE WALL - (PROJECT)
5. DAWN WALL - V3
6. ECLIPSE - (SS) V4
7. SOLAR STORM - (SS) V3

8. ZOMBIE WALL - V2
9. ZOMBIE GROOVE - V3
10. COP OUT - V3
11. KILLER WEED - V4
12. TOMBSTONE WALL (PROJECT)

13. EAST WALL - V0
14. CORTEGE NOIR- V3 (SS V6)
15. RUDEBOY TRAVERSE - V7
16. PALLBEARER WALL - V2
17. CORTEGE CRACK - V3

18. THUG LIFE ARETE - V3

STONE COUNTRY TOPOS

'Death and Ben Ledi'

'Ben Ledi is a devil's punchbowl hill just north of the Flanders Moss and Stirlingshire wheat fields, inhabited by pinnacles and boulders and some unfortunate history. In the 19th Century, a funeral party, crossing over the pass to St Bride's Chapel in midwinter, broke through the treacherous ice of Lochan nan Corp ('The Loch of Corpses'), and drowned most of the local clan. This knowledge, along with the tombstone-like boulders and gargoyle pinnacles on the north-eastern slopes of this hill, provides a gothic backdrop to bouldering despite such a brochure outlook to the east. On a late summer afternoon, with the heather bloody and vibrant, and the problems highball enough to feel your mortality quicken, the theme of darkness seems out of place for such an activity, but in essence climbing is always about death. The fear of falling, the sudden abilities found not to fall, are animal reactions to the genetic inheritance called vertigo. God is invoked (the Gaelic name Ledi refers to the Beltane Festival Gods) as you climb, if not reverently. The problems are by their nature close to being dangerous, almost routes in fact, but sometimes you have to go beyond the happy motion of the physical and get a little more metaphysical, in a sense moving when failure to do so matters gravely. Clinging hard to mica-schist crimps, praying they won't snap; reaching high like penitents for a thank-God hold to finish with, always fearful that there will be no good finishing hold at all, like there might be no afterlife. You feel all this in a kind of miniature panic until it focuses all you know about ascending and then it is over, this little death, at least until the next boulder.'

Left to right:
1. Steve Richardson on 'Weeping Wall'.
2. The Sunstone.
3. Reaching high on 'The Pallbearer'.

54

BEN LEDI BOULDERING

From Stirling follow the A84 and signs for Callander. Continue through the town and up the winding road by the Falls of Leny. When this flattens out, take a sudden left-hand metal bridge to parking. A flat kilometre walk north leads to a steep way-marked path up through the forests into Stank Glen. Follow the corrie path to where the pinnacles come into view up on the left. From a white marker post and low boulder, follow a small burn up to a sudden plateau, where the huge boulders come into view. A good warm-up walk with a boulder mat!

The lowest climbable 'Corpse' boulder over on the right facing up to the pinnacles provides some good warm-up problems:

Corpse Arête - The terrific north-west arête can be climbed on either side depending on nerve... the left side is slightly harder.

Weeping Wall - On the south side of this boulder (facing uphill) there is a good green wall which can be climbed direct using an undercut to the distant horizontal break.

Just up from this boulder is the prowed boulder of the 'Sunstone':

Eclipse - The sit-down to the prow itself is a powerful problem climbing the curving prow on pockets to a hopeful lunge for jugs.

Solar Storm - Climbs the back wall just right of Eclipse.

Dawn Wall - The left hand hanging corner and Africa-shaped flake is best climbed by pressing into the square-cut wee corner, then undercut up and left to a spike. Work back right into the top of the corner to finish on pockets and better holds up and left - an excellent excursion requiring patience to find the right positions and holds.

Sunstone Wall - The broken flake on the right is now a desperate project.

The big boulders just above the fence are disappointing, but there is one very obvious challenge – the *Tombstone Roof* . This project aims to climb the leaning wall and escape round the roof leftwards at pockets.

The pale-skinned boulder of the 'Moonstone' sits in the middle of the main boulders and gives some good highball problems on its downhill face:

Zombie Groove - The flaky-looking groove is more solid than it looks.

Zombie Wall - Clims the excellent highball wall direct.

Cop Out Arête - The hanging prow, steady all the way after a steep start.

Killer Weed - The capped overhang starts sitting just left of the Cop-Out problem and breaks up and left on crimps to slopers on the lip, to pull over rightwards. Descend by the crack. Body tension is the key.

The 'Cortège Boulder' has an uphill vertical west wall and overhanging south wall. It offers some of the best rock and problems in this boulderfield, technically demanding and powerful to boot.

Cortège Crack - This takes the left hand seam crack and is twisty and reachy, so don't warm up on it.

Pallbearer - The middle of the wall is climbed to good central holds, then stretches up to the top. The right arête is the descent route.

Rudeboy - This excellent problem traverses rightwards from the descent arête on edges to gain a sloper, which in good conditions might gain more sharp holds to a crimp sloper, from where an exciting jump gains jugs high on the right arête.

Cortège Noir - The sitting start to the right-hand side of the wall. Undercuts from the arête up left to a big sidepull, then press into a flat crimp. Sidepress the undercut to the left, which might help gain a high right crimp to rock up to the jugs on the arête, or simply Kung-Fu it to finish!

Thug Life - The arête on the wee boulder up from the Cortège boulder.

The Corpse Boulder.

Glen Lednock clockwise:

1. Niall Howett, Chris Duffy, Rory Howett and Liam Duffy (climbing) on 'Kids' Stuff!'
2. Rory Howett on 'Billy No Clan'
3. 'Smoothie'
4. Kev Howett on 'Elizabethan Chorus'

'Kids' Stuff'

"In Perthshire, near the town of Comrie, is a gorgeous glen called Glen Lednock. The biggest thing there is a huge dam which stands approximately one hundred feet high and is for hydro electric. There are also quite a few boulders below the dam, in fact the whole hillside is covered in big jumbles of boulders and in the summer the high bracken means we can have great fun exploring and scrambling too.

I started bouldering here in 2001 when my Dad realized that a lot of the boulders are really good for kids. The first ever boulder problem I did at Glen Lednock was with my dad. While he was trying some hard overhanging new problems I did a problem on the 'Taper Slab' which was not too hard. We started going a lot more in the summer holidays in 2003 and I did a lot more bouldering. I did one problem on a boulder called The Pyramid. This I called *Smoothie*, because all the holds are rounded - my brother Niall seemed to find it easier to run up it without using his hands. When we went there the next time he was inclined to do it again this way and I tried it too and I did find it easier. Then we started to go with the next-door neighbours (Chris, Carl and Liam) who had never climbed before and they enjoyed it.

The next big boulder we discovered was the 'Riever's Stone'. The first problem I did on it is called *There and Back Again* and is always a good one to start on. It climbs the biggest face of the boulder and is like a small route. Niall also did a problem here, which is the route we use to get down, but its much harder climbing up it!

The Drover's Trail is the second one I did. It is always good fun and I usually warm up on its easy slab. The best boulder problem I am going to tell you about is the hardest I have ever done. I called it *Billy no Clan*. It was about the fifth problem I had ever done. It starts under a roof under the boulder. You have to grab two handholds in a diagonal crack in the lip and get support for your feet underneath the boulder, then heel-hook the sloping ledge on the arête. It's a tough pull up to get both hands on the higher hand-holds in the crack before you have to step-up. You follow the crack up to the arête and finish off with delicate climbing up that.

Apart from the superb bouldering, the things that attracted me to the glen are the beautiful scenery, the river where we paddle and the waterfalls and deep pools where we also dive, swim and go snorkelling. It's a great place."

Rory Howett - 2004

Rory Howett on 'Tomb Raiders'

'A River Runs Through It'

"You have spent a week accumulating aggression, tension, intolerance and selfishness... something has curdled your karma. Your head is in bad shape. You register the tautness in your back and neck. So...you go for a walk in the wild country and after an hour's serious uphill trudge you stumble across what appears to be a prime bouldering spot: a cluster of craglets and big free-standing boulders, with a heartbreakingly beautiful view. Great rock, problems from V-easy to V-hard, with the boulders identifiable by the tree each of them has growing at the bottom – a rowan, a yew, a banyan tree and a coconut palm (ok, ok, that was just to see if you were still with me). It's one of the nicest spots you've ever been to. You're in love. A river runs through it. The river was spawned by the great Ocean and runs over rocks that cooled in the cradle of Pre-Cambrian time. You spend an age carving your dreams on the stone. In your sleep, you mime the moves of the problems you can't yet do. You vow to train for them, individually if necessary. All good things – fine boulder problems as well as spiritual enlightenment – come by grace and grace comes by art and art does not come easy.

Two weeks, and you've been getting obsessive again, training, getting it wired, getting strong. You feel your fingers tingling with the rock's imprint, synapses still sizzling from the physics of the moves. Up in Glen X, your highball project is waiting, a fine line slicing the Highland sky like a scalpel; a fine line between success and injury. You take a two day city break for the rest and then go to three for the psyche, keeping your weather eye open. You can when you live close. Back at the big boulder, washed and blown dry by a brisk cold wind, you visualize those moves that were so totally, so absolutely out of the question on your first visit. The grain of the rock, its curve and colour become your whole focus as you build your dreams around the magnificent obsession that by some miracle of soul control you can choreograph the sequence and get it right this time.

Rehearsals are over; it's Showtime, time to suspend disbelief, time to mobilize, focus, reach out past what is normal and perform. Even the chill glen plays along, gleaming improbably phosphorescent and silent as a concert hall as you breathe and concentrate, eyes closing, zoning in, processing *ki* energy and power. Eyes closed now, breathing in and out through the nose, memory mimes the moves as you generate symbiosis of stillness and movement before the big release...

Chalk, blow and go...

And it is hard, but today it is controlled and you are good and sharp and strong and the moves build fast as you hook the arête and pop for the intermediate to kill the swing and stretch on through for the ridiculous pinch. Glancing down – bad move – you see the cruel, chaotic jumble of rocks framing the sloping mortuary slab below. Up and to the right, you view in a split second the crucial non-hold, the one you have invested with a gruesome personality all of its own. Crunch time. Foot on the high smear, other leg flagged out, you slap rightwards, catch the hold and nearly corkscrew off before tensing and holding the body position to make the second slap accurately enough to share on the hold from hell. Cutting loose now, you pull so hard on that hold that your teeth bleed, howling your delight across the glen as you foot-hunt the dish by the pinch, nail it and grab the top.

Back at the car and proud of your recklessness, you sigh into the driver's seat as the first drops of rain patter on the roof like hairpins dropping into a plastic cup. As you watch the rain, the cleansing process has begun. The bile and vitriol have gone. You feel unreal again. On the drive home you wind down the windows to give your smile room..."

Tim Carruthers 2004

'TC' on 'Tsunami' - V9 - Glen Lednock

'Weem Dream'

"Time spent at Weem's bouldering wall is always refreshing, not least because of the highball nature of the thing, although mats have made the difference here from possible E grade to only V grade. The lines too are surprisingly well defined for a flat wall. Despite only appearing vertical, the holds are small and poor enough to make it acceptably hard, and with all the starts undercut by a small roof covered in good holds, the transition from horizontal to vertical is akin to those horrible final moves encountered on bulges of ice. Dispensing with the obvious upward lines barring one, I brought in more muscle in the form of Tim Carruthers. In so doing, we inadvertently pieced together the start for the traverse of the lip of the roof and not long after, stringing it together became a slight obsession. I often name problems before they are complete to help focus the mind on getting it done and this name seemed to sum it up perfectly. Like an impecunious youth being problematical in class, 'Getting Lippy' finally succumbed to my wishes after a prolonged verbal onslaught.

'The Chop': I lay underneath its initial roof on numerous occasions and tried to pull onto the barely there crimps on the wall above but getting my bum off the ground even felt hard. A few more visits and I could at least do that vicious start. Strangely, it succumbed by surprise, at a time when I was recovering from a landscape gardening injury (don't go there!). Suddenly I was on the crimps, my feet subconsciously fell onto the right holds to make it possible and I was slapping for the bigger holds. It happened so fast I can't remember much about it and as the only witness on the day, my ever faithful dog, was asleep in the sun I had no-one to share the moment with either."

Kevin Howett - 2004

'Getting Lippy' - Weem Bouldering Wall

Kev Howett on 'The Chop', Weem.

Clach Druim A Charn

Roof Boulder

Hero Stone

ARRAN
GRANITE BOULDERS

(OS MAP 69 - NOT TO SCALE)

CAT STONE (GR 020 443)

1. BOLT HOLE SLAB - V0
2. ROAD WALL - V0
3. ROAD WALL 2 - V2
4. ROADKILL ARETE - V0
5. DESCENT ROUTE - V0
6. THE BULGE PROJECT

7. HERO SLAB - V0
8. HERO ARETE - V2
9. THE SCOOP - V2

10. DHRUIM CRACK - V0
11. SCOOP SLAB - V0
12. WEST WALL CRACK - V3

13. RIGHT ROOF
14. LEFT ROOF

O UNCLIMBED LINES

SANNOX

STONE COUNTRY TOPOS

THE FIRTH OF CLYDE

HERO STONE (GR 023 439)

GOATFELL   CORRIE

CLACH DHRUIM A CHARN (GR 025 419)

ROOF BOULDER (GR 025 418)

P

BRODICK

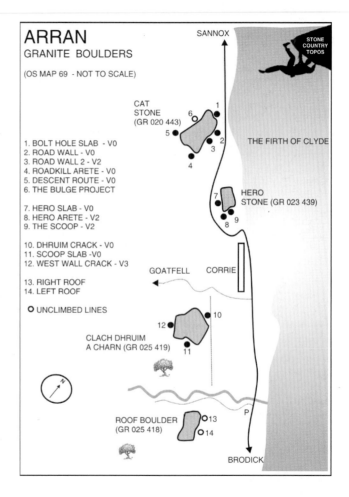

THE HERO STONES OF ARRAN

If you are kipping on your mate's sofa in Glasgow, and have been battered by the precision and dedication required at Dumbarton, there is a local venue in a lost world of granite giants not a morning's travel from the choke of the city: the Isle of Arran. In the summer, the early train catches the 7am ferry and by eight, full of galley chips and beans, you can buy an Island-Rover ticket, skip on the north circular bus from Brodick harbour and hop off at Corrie with the walkers heading up Goatfell. Shrug off the comments about your boulder mat and head up to one of the many granite boulders round the village. South of Corrie, a hundred yards from the road is the Clach Mhor Druim a' Charn - a big, slabbed boulder with a scooped crack in it, providing a steep back wall and good landings. Further south, two hundred yards, and right above a layby, is a steeper roofed boulder with some excellent hard problems. After an hour or so on these stones, you can walk north towards Sannox and play on the roadside boulders of Clach an Fhionn (the Hero Stone) or the bigger Cat Stone, plonked on a bend of the road, where any dismounts must be carefully timed not to catapult you into the astonished path of a touring car. But that is not all there is to Arran bouldering: the big glens hide some mighty boulders and where you can grow strong as a hero on mountain water and granite bouldering. Glen Catacol has some good bouldering as well, and in the east are the Machrie Moor stones: not for climbing on, but for absorbing the meaning we find in large stones, and for contemplating the long link between more ancient lithophiles and ourselves. In the south, Kildonan has some fine bouldering on scooped and gnarled gabbro by the shore, and, to complete the circuit, there is secret sandstone bouldering in the rhododendron darkness of Merkland wood in the grounds of Brodick castle. Grades are an irrelevance here on this island and constant movement is the key. A mat is not even a necessity as landings are usually dry and grassy - it is a land of the solo climber, of standing on your Buffalo jacket, going native, becoming the hero of the stones, meditating over the crystal cuts in the quicks of your fingers, and focusing deep on the loneliness and natural joy of climbing.

For the dedicated boulderer on Arran, the most promising (though possibly the most distracting) bouldering lies on the alp below Cir Mhor, under the sweeping slabs in the Fhionn Coire basin. A long trek up the path in Glen Rosa leads to a left turn up into the high corrie below the very alpine exposure of clean granite on the Rosa Pinnacle. As the path levels out after a steep climb, a picnic plinth of rock lies by the path up to the obvious saddle in the A'Chir ridge. From this stone a plethora of boulders can be seen on the grassy alp below the main faces and behind, across a small gorge southwards. Many hard projects and unclimbed features remain, but the natural lines on these boulders provide superb granite bouldering with very good grassy landings. The bouldering is largely on clean compact rock and is largely unclaimed, though some dramatic bouldering lines stand out. There are fine bivi spots, so out of midge season (June-August) a sleeping bag and stove can be stuffed in a boulder mat and, provided you can resist the temptation of the big routes, you can spend a weekend plucking problems from these great stones.

Bouldering on the Cat Stone, Arran.

Gneiss: the oldest rock on the planet. Found on the fringes of the north west and the Hebrides, some of it is at least a dizzying 2000 million years old. Can be climbed on at The Ruthven Boulder, Morar (opposite), Butt of Lewis, Shetland and Wester Ross.

The House Boulder, Glen Massan. Mica Scist. A ubiquitous rock in the Southern and Central Highlands, it was formed under the metamorphic pressures of the 'Caledonian Orogeny', about 400 million years ago. The rock is folded and scalloped, sometimes compact and pocketed, and heavily gemmed with quartz and garnet.

The Kishorn Boulder, Applecross. Torridonian Sandstone. Around 700 million years old, this un-fossilled sandstone boulder was once part of a pebbled red delta from a vanished continent until carved into its present shape and set on view by a glacier.

The Gabbro of Skye. A compass-spinning rock and another superb vulcaneous example of the Tertiary period, it is rough and rasping, providing superb friction but somewhat painful! Boulders can be found on Skye, Mull and Ardnamurchan.

The Cat Stone on Arran has been blasted, then circumvented by a road due to its size. Formed of granite from the more violent eruptions and magma swellings during the tertiary period, it's a a mere 65 million years old.

Dolerite. The heaviest, densest rock cooled from volcanic vents and plugs and dykes, its best boulders are undoubtedly at Dumbarton Rock. Can be found throughout Central Scotland and the Clyde hills. Provides both sloping and angular fractured rock, at first confusing and much like climbing a Picasso painting.

Precious Cargo

"Five days ago, early Monday morning, the earth was a roaring molten whirlpool in space, slowly solidifying throughout the day into a fiery orbit round a young sun. Scotland was nothing but a fretful dream of fire. On Tuesday, the rock began to cool and form vague continents under lightning clouds and hot rain. The seas boiled and steamed with unknowable events. By Wednesday, the Earth had decided to build some foundations to a geological folly: the Hebrides had its base of Lewisian Gneiss laid down along with the oldest rocks of Greenland. Thursday came and great dust storms arrived to cover all these old rocks with an arid red carpet and the birth of Torridon was whispered in the heat. Friday morning - today - was the turn of the great oceans, which rippled over vast continents, teeming with soupy life, laying down muds and dead things which would be metamorphosed into Schists and Quartzite's and Slates: you could say we're bouldering on our ancestors. Then at noon – high noon – came the time of mountain building. Scotland (part of the vast continent of Laurentia), squeezed out the Iapetus Ocean to meet the northwards drifting Avalonia (England) and all hell broke loose. Mountain masses boiled up – the Cairngorm plateau reared out of softer rocks like a great bald granite head – sea-beds were warped and lifted and volcanoes exploded and leaked everywhere: the whole crush of the Scottish highlands took basic shape against the forcing ground of the Highland Boundary fault. Then, by early afternoon, it all quietened down again. Shallow seas rose and fell, the air was tropical and life burgeoned and splashed and climbed out of the sea while Scotland sweated on the equator. It was not until about an hour ago – after a brief diversion with dinosaurs – when things began to heat up again: the land rose from its chalky seas and great volcanoes spouted and laid down Gabbros and Basalts and Granites. America and Greenland drifted away and the mountainous identity of Scotland reared up through the softer rocks. It was in this time we witnessed the noisy birth of great boulders on Skye and Rum and Arran. As for the rest of the last hour, it was quiet, but for the persistent whisper of erosion. Wind and rain and tropical rivers etched away at the raw layers of Scotland until, quite suddenly, about three minutes ago, the ice arrived. We had drifted too far north and found ourselves smothered by a deep crush of ice, which tore its way over a new land, bearing our boulders and scouring out huge corries. And then, just before midnight, a tenth of a second ago, the ice melted and revealed its precious cargo of stones - and here they lie, exiled to the light, the air, the wind, and the rather sudden laying on of respectful, chalky hands."

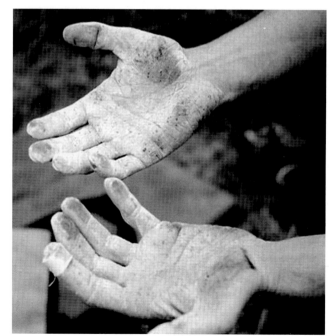

Googling the Tarken Stone

"Not much comes up, I click on a link: *Standing Stones, Ley Lines and Power Points:*

Known as the The Rocking Stone of Glen Tarken, this huge boulder, like a facetted diamond in the centre of a number of ley lines, reputedly once rocked in a high wind, possibly to alter their wavelengths (straight ley lines are streams of vertical waves with a wavelength of 5 - 6 ft). Now it is as motionless as the hills themselves.

Woahhhhh horsey! Was I harnessing the ancient telluric energy of ley lines? I had seen a picture of the Tarken Stone, an awesome boulder on the Perthshire heather high above St Fillans. The only search on Google found this stone had its own followers of modern ancients and a panic welled up - would I be stamping all over their heritage, what would I say if I met them? What would they think? Blinking, looking at me clinging on to his stone like some demented lemur.

The stone weighs 162 pounds per cubic foot and is hundreds of millions of years old, so much dense ignorance you wonder it cares, let alone resonates with our presence. It is massive, birthed from a schist crag, exiled on its own, maybe by some ancient glacier, with a pathetic heather cap to keep the weather off. It overhangs on three sides and feels like it could screw with your compass. I hunker under it from a sudden squall and think about the ley lines warping and shifting through its mass, like some invisible gut. Maybe we boulderers have our own ley lines of wonder, connecting all great bouldering stones. Maybe that line runs right through us all, a skewer of desire, a climbing lust that grips your belly internally when you see new stones.

I ask the local farmer about it on the way down and he looks at me unmoved, his crook pinning down a knackered ewe, 'Aye, that'll be it, the rocking stone'. I tell him I'd been climbing on it. 'It's supposed to move in a high wind, eh?' I say. 'Aye, mibbe,' he mutters. He sparks up a full strength Marlboro and sniffs – this either means nothing to him, or he considers me a nutter, walking into a remote glen to clamber on a boulder, surely I could find something better to do? But I can't and we talk about sane things: the mild weather, the spawning frogs, the 'blue hare' which I thought was white. I walk away, still feeling the big internal tug of the Tarken Stone, happy in my madness, waiting for it to pull me back like the invisible elastic band of the ley-lines."

Four scarred flamingoes!

'Finger-licker', Cummingston.

Portlethen Prow, the Sea-Pig.

Glen Nevis, clockwise from left:

1. Jo George on the Cameron Stone
2. Sky-Pilot area
3. 'Silver Slab'

Clockwise from left:

1. 'Bright-Sized life' - Glen Nevis
2. Cubby bouldering at Sky-Pilot
3. Hats off on the Scimitar

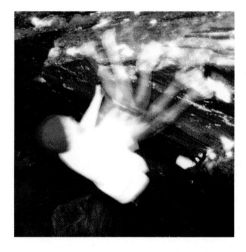

'Otter Wall', Beasdale, Morar.

"The mind has mastery over the body and knows it. In such moments all a man's diffidence about his own capacities is cast off: all his lack of push, due to uncertainty of his powers, is replaced by a singleness of purpose, from which springs strenuousness and real powers of initiative."

W.H.Murray -
'Mountaineering in Scotland'

Mal Meech adventure bouldering on Skye.

"In both bouldering and mathematics, you stand upon the threshold of something new, something that requires not only brute force (whether it be physical or intellectual force) but a certain insight, a certain quantum jump from point to point."

John Gill – 'Master of Rock'

'Physical Graffiti', Dumbarton.

Gary Vincent on Eagle Rock, Dumbarton.

"Great eggs of time. The rock is unknowably old. You can't get your head round how old this stone must be. Abandoned by time, a legacy of an ancient glacier's ice-clad dreams, they demand a hearing. It might seem overblown to regard these stones too much, if it were not for the time they hold clenched in their loneliness. To lay hands on the stones, to climb them, is to revere more than stone itself, to move with more than just muscles and bone through the invisible net of weight - it is the gravity well of time itself we ascend. It is when confronted by great, isolated stones where we find our reasons to climb focused, ground down to a conceptual lens, a clear point made by a dark stone. It is why I would maintain that it is the boulderer who can understand time through stone, as much as the mountaineer apprehends the ancient in the mountain."

James Sutton on 'Snake Attack', Sron na Ciche, Skye.

The Beasdale Boulder, Morar.

Mike Tweedley on 'Precious', Arrochar.

Dave MacLeod on the awesome 'Sabotage', Dumbarton.

Tim Moroozo at the Thirlstane, Dumfries.

"... the Narnain Boulders are the best quality bouldering you'll get in Arrochar - the rock is perfection (for mica schist that is...)"

Niall McNair

Niall McNair on his Narnain project.

Graham MacBirnie on Mull: 'Pain is weakness leaving the body...'

MULLED GABBRO

Mull is a great volcanic island, with shields of basalt layered like pie-crusts and a core of harder, older granites and gabbros. Fionnphort, the ferry-point to Iona on the Ross of Mull, has fine bouldering on lovely pink granite walls, but probably the best bouldering on Mull is located in the delightful haven of Loch Buie, tucked away under its own private mountain in the south-east of Mull. This was once a boiling pit of gabbro-spitting magma. The boulders here reflect the texture and pressure of volcanism; roughly skinned like solidified pumice. Here and there the rock is smoother, pitted by wind and salt-air into bubbled popcorn shapes and like a sticky-handed kid, you just want to put your chalky paws on the candy - the boulders naturally tease the eye with feature and deceptive simplicity. Set beside tranquil beaches, and sparsely populated, it is a perfect place to bring a boulder mat, and the quality rewards the traveler.

Kirtsty McBirnie on 'The Nose', Loch Buie.

LOCH BUIE
GABBRO BOULDERING

OS MAP 48 (BOULDERS NOT TO SCALE)

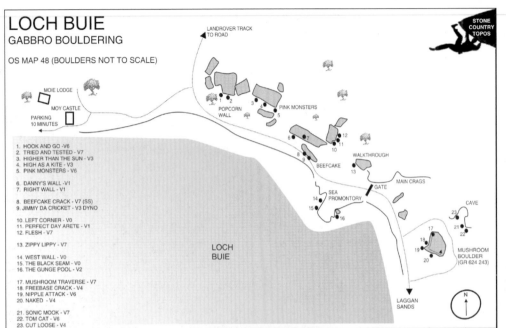

STONE COUNTRY TOPOS

1. HOOK AND GO -V6
2. TRIED AND TESTED - V7
3. HIGHER THAN THE SUN - V3
4. HIGH AS A KITE - V3
5. PINK MONSTERS - V6

6. DANNY'S WALL -V1
7. RIGHT WALL - V1

8. BEEFCAKE CRACK - V7 (SS)
9. JIMMY DA CRICKET - V3 DYNO

10. LEFT CORNER - V0
11. PERFECT DAY ARETE - V1
12. FLESH - V7

13. ZIPPY LIPPY - V7

14. WEST WALL - V0
15. THE BLACK SEAM - V0
16. THE GUNGE POOL - V2

17. MUSHROOM TRAVERSE - V7
18. FREEBASE CRACK - V4
19. NIPPLE ATTACK - V6
20. NAKED - V4

21. SONIC MOOK - V7
22. TOM CAT - V6
23. CUT LOOSE - V4

Clockwise:

1. Nipple Attack, Mushroom Boulder
2. Freebase, Mushroom Boulder
3. Perfect Day Traverse
4. Danny's Wall
5. The Gunge Pool

LOCH BUIE BOULDERING

From Oban, regular ferries sail to Craignure, from where the main road can be taken south for 10k, to a left turn onto a B-road at Strathcoil. This is taken for about 12 kilometres to the shores of the picturesque Loch Buie. From here, a walk eastwards past the gatehouse and along the shore past Moy Castle leads to the crags and boulders by the land-rover track to the big strand of Laggan Sands. If you're on a bike, cut down the track following signs to Laggan Sands B and B, it's a bit quicker. The 'PopCorn Wall' is the first textured wall of the embedded buttress behind the tree.

Hook and Go - Climbs the superb steep arête right of the overhang, using heels and dynamism!

Tried and Tested - Takes the popcorned right wall direct on small crimps and pockets.

The Pink Monsters Boulder' lies just to the right, behind the rhododendron screen.

Higher than the Sun - The central left line is steady but highball.

High as a Kite - The line just right again.

Pink Monsters - The best problem on this wall, it is a technical hanging arête which is very hard to get established on and crimpy to the top. Likely to strip the skin, as it suggests.

'The Perfect Day Boulder' is the boulder with the square-cut corner on the right, viewed from the track. The problems are on the right hand east wall.

The Corner - Good climbing up the wee corner to a flat top.

Perfect Day - Takes the arête just to the right of the corner.

Flesh - Another sacrificial climb! Takes the central wall on painful crimps and usually involves long immersion in confusion and pain before success.

'The Beefcake Boulder' overhangs the track.

Beefcake - The obvious crack from a difficult sit-down start.

Jimmy da Cricket - Just left of the above problem, dyno from crimps to the top.

Just behind this is the beautifully pockmarked 'Danny's Wall', with a wee cave embedded in it.

Danny's Wall - This takes the obvious overhanging flakes on the left of the wee cave, with a puzzling top-out, excellent rock and great climbing!

Right Wall - Traverses along the cave to climb the high thin crack on good holds, an excellent introduction to the secure nature of Loch Buie gabbro.

'The Walk-Through Boulder' is the next big boulder you can walk underneath!

Zippy Lippy - The only line so far, by Mike Tweedley, it is a traverse along the slopey lip rightwards to exit above the walk-through. The cave has a seam of basalt running through it, which might provide holds for a strong climber to pull out into the light.

In front of this boulder is the 'Sea Promontory' with enjoyable west, east and south walls.

West Wall - Up the undercuts on the left, veering right to jugs.

Black Seam - A difficult start gains the left edge of the seam.

The seaward wall has a good traverse, but the best problem here is:

The Gunge Pool - On the east walls, this travels right from a thigh-height ledge by the obvious nose of rock, crossing through to a pinch and a good slot, from where the tallest part of the wall is climbed. Don't fall in the green gunge. The wee crack is harder.

After this, a gate is crossed, the main crags are passed and the track drops down to the sands, where a squat boulder lies in a fenced-off field in front of a cave. 'The Mushroom Boulder' is the gem of Loch Buie.

The Mushroom Traverse - This works left to right around the boulder to finish standing on the slopey ledge.

Freebase - Climbs the vague crack line left of the nose, from a sitting start at frustrating slopers. If you can do this move, the rest follows easily up the nose.

Nipple Attack - Superb climbing fom a sit-start under the nose at a crimp-rail, yarding out left to a left-hand crimp and a slopey boss, where a desperate horizontal twist and slap might gain the finishing holds.

Naked - This climbs straight through the crimped front roof from a sitting start.

The cave had some excellent problems as well, such as:

Cut Loose - Climbs from the back of the shelf to a good hold on the arête, cuts loose and climbs to the top.

Sonic Mook - On the right side of the cave. An impressive arête which is climbed from a low start and long reach with the left hand, then heel hooks allow technical progress to be made all the way up.

Tom Cat - Just to the right of the arête, climb up into the groove via an undercut and sloper on the bulge.

'The Morrighan', Glen Nevis.

HEATHER HATS AND SCIMITARS

Glen Nevis is one of the most dramatic glens in the Highlands, cradling boulders chipped from its great heights and crags. Waking groggy from a tent in the early spring, with the mist rolling off the awesome Ben and the roar of the gorge, you might be mistaken for being in the Alps. The place is a haven for craggers, for the schist rock provides fine quality slabs and walls and snaking cracks and skull-shaped crags amongst other features. Not only is it a climber's paradise, but also a boulderer's. There is simply so much un-documented bouldering that the ethic would be to leave it that way, but there are some boulders, recently developed and cleaned, plucked from their introspection, that are worth revealing to the world, such as the 'Heather Hat', 'The Scimitar', the 'Cameron Stone'. The rock is a rough, bubbly schist, which shears to give smooth slopers or tiny crimps, but its natural texture is generous and some problems require no chalk on the fingers at all. The best time to visit is a bright breezy day in high summer, when the midges are quiet, or in spring and autumn when the rock is cooler and the flying sharks are asleep or dead in the grass. The glen is superb for exploring and simply a matter of finding yourself a boulder in the woods or on one of the many alps and bringing a keen eye and a child's nose for the cookie jar... there is good bouldering at all grades, projects for the bouldering specialist and fine pools to swim in at the end of a summer's day.

The Scimitar

GLEN NEVIS
SCHIST BOULDERS

OS MAP 41 (BOULDERS NOT TO SCALE)

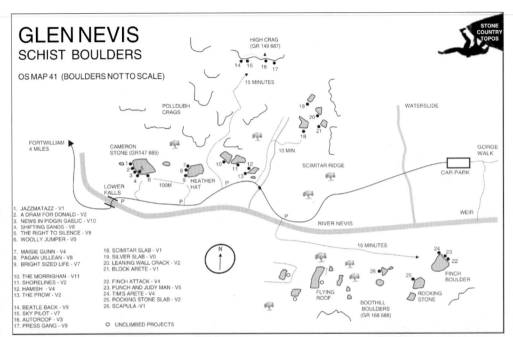

HIGH CRAG
(GR 149 687)

14 15   16   17

15 MINUTES

POLLDUBH
CRAGS

WATERSLIDE

19
20
18   21

FORTWILLIAM
4 MILES

CAMERON
STONE (GR147 685)

10 MIN.

GORGE
WALK

SCIMITAR RIDGE

CAR PARK

1
2
3   5
4   6

7
8
9 HEATHER
     HAT

10
11   12
13

100M

LOWER
FALLS

WEIR

RIVER NEVIS

15 MINUTES

24   23
22

FINCH
BOULDER

26

25

FLYING
ROOF

ROCKING
STONE

BOOTHILL
BOULDERS
(GR 168 688)

N

1. JAZZMATAZZ - V1
2. A DRAM FOR DONALD - V2
3. NEWS IN PIDGIN GAELIC - V10
4. SHIFTING SANDS - V8
5. THE RIGHT TO SILENCE - V8
6. WOOLLY JUMPER - V0

7. MAISIE GUNN - V4
8. PAGAN UILLEAN - V8
9. BRIGHT SIZED LIFE - V7

10. THE MORRIGHAN - V11
11. SHORELINES - V2
12. HAMISH - V4
13. THE PROW - V2

14. BEATLE BACK - V9
15. SKY PILOT - V7
16. AUTOROOF - V3
17. PRESS GANG - V9

18. SCIMITAR SLAB - V1
19. SILVER SLAB - V0
20. LEANING WALL CRACK - V2
21. BLOCK ARETE - V1

22. FINCH ATTACK - V4
23. PUNCH AND JUDY MAN - V5
24. TIM'S ARETE - V4
25. ROCKING STONE SLAB - V2
26. SCAPULA -V1

O   UNCLIMBED PROJECTS

Clockwise:

1. Sean Culpan on 'Woolly Jumper'
2. 'Finch Attack'
3. 'Flying Roof' at Boothill
4. The Cameron Stone
5. 'Tim's Arete', Boothill Boulders

86

GLEN NEVIS BOULDERING

On the road north out of Fortwilliam, turn off to the sign-posted Glen Nevis and follow this all the way up to the higher glen for a few miles where the Polldubh crags become visible. Cross the bridge over the River Nevis lower falls. The first boulder soon appears up on the left, a hundred yards from the road. This is the mighty 'Cameron Stone'. The main boulders are all accessible from the wee lay-by car-park below this boulder. For the Boothill boulders, the car-park at the road-head by the gorge is the best access point in the summer, when the river is low and can be crossed easily, but if it's in spate approach via the bridge and path by the River Nevis, at the midway bend in the road.

The 'Cameron Stone' is the big leaning boulder perched over a spring. Strong fingers are a necessity! The best problems on this stone are: *Jazzmatazz* which climbs from the flat sloper straight up on good holds. *A Dram for Donald* starts from the same low ledge on the face pointing down the glen, then takes crimps rightwards to better holds and a direct mantel finish. *The News in Pidgin Gaelic for White Settlers* takes the awesome steep wall from under the roof at an undercut, thereafter struggling on small crimps to the top. The arête itself can be climbed and bear-hugged on crimps aiming for the jug, to give *Shifting Sands*. The front face has the delightful high crackline of *Woolly Jumper* difficult to start and finishing out right with exposure. *The Right to Silence* starts at the cave's jug rail and foot-locks up left, where crimps can be found on the arête, then moves right onto the crimpy wall to finish. *Right Arête* is the obvious warm-up for this boulder, gaining the cracked nose to finish.

The 'Heather Hat' is a stone for the primates. On the same contour line as the Cameron Stone, this has a wild and obvious roof over a plinth of stone. The left hand roof-line is the magnificent *Maisie Gunn* - a wondrous tour out from the back left of the roof, to the nose and up the left arête, usually perma-chalked. Just to the right is the main roof line of *Pagan Uilleann*, giving hard and bizarre climbing out along the obvious cracked roof block to mantel over the centre. To the right again, is another tremendous problem: *Bright Size Life* which takes the right-hand roof from the quartz hold, gaining poor slopers under the roof, then an undercut near the right edge. From here, sort the feet and lunge for the good lip holds, where the best finish rocks out right to a small undercut. Variations of this can be done depending on your lust for elimination. The traverse of the whole hanging lip from right to left is *Midnight in a Perfect World (V6)* finishing up the mantel of Maisie Gunn.

The 'Morrighan Block' is the impending roof hidden under the crag of Pinnacle Ridge, a couple of hundred yards up from the Heather Hat. *The Morrighan* is the challenge of the leaning wall. Sit start from a pinched side-pull and edge, snatch desperately for the next thumby crimp, from where a couple of moves gain an incut hold just under the right arête. Finish by gaining the wee horizontal crack and layback up the arête, if you somehow find yourself there...

The 'Heart Stone' is the obvious grooved boulder facing towards the road, above the Standing Stone. Its main wall has the good *Crack and Slab* on the left and a tremendous highball scooped groove in the centre: *Shorelines*.

The 'Standing Stone' is the obvious prowed boulder seen from the road lies below the Morrighan Block complex. *Hamish* - look round the back of the prow! From the small undercuts slap up left for a small hold, a right crimp, then aim for better holds. The sit-down crimping out right is *MacTavish (V9)*. Most strikingly, *The Prow* takes the nose direct from a sitting start.

'The Scimitar' is the obvious jagged boulder underneath Scimitar crag, in the next wee glen with a burn running under the road, about ten minutes from the road. *Scimitar Slab* is the superb cracked, tapering slab and can be climbed direct to layback and smear up the left edge to a crux at the top - the sloping right edge is a red herring all the way. Off to the right, under the crag, are further boulders. The lowest block has an excellent *Left Edge*, mantelling up right onto the textured wall, then balancing up left to finish. The next boulder has a clean-cut steep face. *Leaning Crack* is the right-hand line of incut jugs leading to a snatch for the apex jugs and easy mantel. The obvious gleaming boulder is the excellent highball *Silver Slab*, the difficulty lying pleasantly at the bottom.

'Sky Pilot Wall'. Not a boulder, but a tremendous bouldering area on a grassy alp under the roof of the skull-shaped High Crag. Hard to describe the approach, but it's a pleasant stomp up through the crags - aim for the 'skull'. The best of the hard problems were created by 'Cubby' and Dave MacLeod. From left to right: *Beatle Back* is a traverse from an obvious pedestal along the break rightwards, to drop down to a lower shelf towards the crack of Sky Pilot, then it continues another five metres to finish up 'Auto-Roof'. *Sky Pilot* is a good sit-start problem under the fault in the centre of the wall. Climb up and left past hand jams then back right on slopers to the niche and then left to jump-off jugs. *Auto Roof* provides easier climbing to a sidepull and then an undercut, to gain the jump-off niche jugs six metres right of Sky Pilot. *Press Gang (V10)* on the far right of the roof is a small left facing corner. From a sit-start to the left, press up to an undercut pinch, then slap for the slots above. Finish at a good quartz hold over the next bulge. The corner is out of bounds.

The 'Boothill Boulders' are the boulders in the field directly across the river from the gorge car-park. In dry conditions the river is easily passable at the old weir. Don't attempt it in spate weather – the boulders will be wet anyway. They can also be approached by walking in from the halfway bridge down the glen. The most easterly boulder - 'The Finch Boulder' - lies near the old weir by the river. *Finch Attack* is the obvious cleaned overhang facing up towards the gorge. From slopers for hands and feet, gain a sharp crimp, aim for holds up and left, then use a remarkable sequence to statically gain the finishing jug up on the right. The undercling challenge to the right, reaching round and up for the top, is *Punch and Judy Man*. Just to the right is *Tim's Arête* which gains and climbs the hanging arête using long reaches.

The 'Rocking Stone' boulder is the slabbed rock behind the Finch boulder. The bulging slab can be climbed in the middle with delicate strength to give *Rocking Stone Slab*. Directly across from the waterslide are two twin boulders, the riverside one having the delightfully textured west face groove of *Scapula*. Further along past some Scots Pines lies a cluster of boulders under Boothill crag. The 'Flying Roof' boulder, by the obvious tree, has the dramatic project which dyno's up left with full commitment to the lip jug - it is desperately hard to stop the self-generated helicoptering.

STONE POETRY

Like a laden ant I weave quickly through long grasses
Mat on back, shoes clenched in fist
Hands chalked in anticipation.
I wade across the river, scrabble up its bank
And there she lies, rudely deposited
At the foot of grand mountain peaks.

For an eternity in their shadow she has lain
And watched a changing world.
I touch her huge grey torso,
Rough and dimpled,
And crimp the deep wrinkles that show her age.
A ripple of quartz leads to shoulders,
Broad and rounded. And on her back
A complex tattoo of mesmerising swirls,
Each one etched by a long moment in time.

With a hot sun pounding my back
For one, two hours I play.
Her intricacies become familiar.
Dry moss clumps tumble to the ground,
And unexpected secrets are revealed.
The vigour of a wire brush improves her complexion,
But after these dormant years,
Have I acted too harshly, or left her scarred?

I lie back exhausted, eyes swollen with lichen dust,
Fingers stinging - and gaze at my creation.
Across her steely grey face
A flurry of bright chalk dabs now scatter
Each dab a move, each move a joy.
In the distant sky a rain cloud forms,
And soon our secret will be washed away,
All evidence gone. One glance back .....

And out of the swirls
I'm sure I see her smile.

Jo George

Boulder Music

Hear the stone that once was hidden
In the glacier's soundless dark.
Observe its short airing
Breach another sea of time.

Our brief excursions, to them
A quiver of moving flesh,
Our fingers, tickling seismometers,
Record them, faint as whalesong.

'Like morality, mountaineering ethics looks to be a matter of discovery rather than decision, and to some degree always a matter of conscience.'

Rai Gaita – 'Sacred Places'

THE RULES OF BOULDERING

Apart from the obvious – you are not aloud to touch the ground as aid to your ascent – bouldering has a tight knot of ethics, mutually understood and adhered to, so as to keep the prize of completing the problem as invigorating and rewarding as possible. Without ethics, you may as well place a ladder against the boulder (for example, in the Lake District, using The Bowderstone ladder is a particular form of ethical laziness on the part of tourists).

Like any other set of morals, the complexities for the ethically minded climber go as deep as Alice's rabbit-hole. The best way to climb a boulder is to find one yourself, choose a good-looking line which finishes on top of the boulder, (giant-like on top of your own cyclopean mountain top) and then climb the problem, first go, without any aid. The purist might say this should be done *al fresco*, but most of us accept the aids of rubber shoes, chalk-bag and baggy shorts.

But what if the problem has been done and documented by someone else? Then we have the beginnings of what boulderers term 'beta', that is, secondary knowledge beneficial to an ascent. A grade, for example, is 'beta' – in other words, you are told that if you train hard enough, can crank x-x-x on the campus board, then you are well capable of flashing boulder problem X (though success always seems to end up dependent on the more noble elements of style and approach). Chalked-up holds, left by a previous boulderer, are 'beta'. Air-mimed climbing by an enthusiastic accomplice is also 'beta'.

Bouldering might not be so concerned with all this, if it didn't worry us what the whole idea of doing a boulder problem actually means. We literally think this without thinking, for even while bouldering on your own, on virgin boulders, there is a strict ethics at play: you simply cannot cheat yourself. You need these strictures, because you respect the rock and the whole idea of the boulder problem – its whole being is contained in how you approach the climb.

Once you step onto the problem and begin a sequence of movements, you naturally accept the rules of gravity and energy and power – these elements cannot be allowed to change until you are safely perched on top of the problem, looking over the edge, hands on your knees, contemplating the rock. And somehow, the rock also contains all the respect you have discovered for those rules. You know the rock won't change the rules, so you won't either… it's all instinct and conscience.

The Gneiss of Loch nan Uamh.

GOOD VIBRATIONS IN MORAR

'As you pass out of Fortwilliam on the Glenfinnan road, the Ben broods in your rear-view mirrors and the landscape changes to a craggy heathered wilderness, deer signs appear everywhere and the long low light of Loch Shiel stretches away like a silver bar. You can feel remoteness clearing the air as you climb out of Glenfinnan and the promise of virgin rock is keen as the eye is drawn to countless crags and walls around the small rail and road junction that is Lochailort. The wilds of south Morar lie northwards, the pretty peninsula and hidden silver beaches (and Gneiss bouldering) of Ardnish to the south. Just before the road swings inland from the Prince's Cairn, Loch nan Uamh bids you stop to admire the stone and sculpture of time and sea. Gneiss is worn smooth into boiler plates with flat swirls and curves. They look like lithographs for ancient maps, how Scotland once looked, stone maps telling us about the time-delay patience of the world. The pebble beach, surrounded by bouldering diversions, demands moments of climbing reflection, the beauty of the stones bidding you sit like a school-child to absorb the primal lessons of geology. Indeed, without this deep respect for their presence in the world, we would not be true climbers. All boulderers are poets at heart, if they look deep enough, for it is the buried life of movement the climber seeks to unearth. Great poets have found this in stone – Hugh MacDiarmid, the epic Scottish poet of the 20th Century, was humbled 'On a Raised Beach, realizing 'stones are one with the stars' and the 'intense vibration in the stones' is precisely what boulderers find through climbing in such a wilderness.

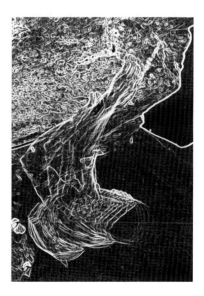

Such poetic moments aside, the boulderer's eye is constantly hunting out Hugh MacDiarmid's 'lithogenesis' and our eyes are drawn up the hill behind this stone museum to a blunt ridge peppered with silhouetted boulders. From Beasdale station, tucked in an icy dark lane of oak and rhododendron, we ploughed up-hill with boulder mats, eyed by a pair of Golden eagles on a small rocky summit, and breasted a rise to find a magnificent flying prowed boulder, an ancient erratic laid down by a glacier against a prop of ground rock, in a manner a boulderer might cry deliberate. Designed to catch the climber's eye it has been scoured clean by bitter winds, its grooves smooth and challenging, its back steep and stooped, its flying prow a wild gesture at the audience of eternal land and sea. The climbing is never desperate, but something wise has informed these remote and hermetic stones. Curious techniques are required: the sudden logic of a palm-down gains height, a toe-hook gains a chalking-up moment of psyched meditation in a wild position, a gyroscopic wobble of doubt on foot friction allows the leg to be straightened, the fingers reaching for the closure of the small summit. The sun sinks into a leaden bank of cloud and we continue pulling on this stone, plucking out its song its stony heart, flushed with the natural poetry of bouldering.'

93

Chris Graham attempting the
desperate Sword project at
the Loch Morar boulders.

LOCH MORAR BOULDERING

Further along the road to Mallaig, a small road turns off eastwards at Morar and winds along the north shore of Loch Morar. At the dead end a few miles later, at Bracorina, a path leads along the shore for two kilometres to a large schist crag overlooking the loch. This is Creag Mhor Bhrinicoire and underneath it is an alp of fine boulders, still awaiting full development. A good mat is required, as well as an assortment of wire brushes, but the rock is solid and many challenging lines remain on these impressive boulders. There are even constructed fishermen bothies under some of the boulders, should you wish to kip the night and swap bouldering tales with fishing tales. The main project line of the obvious 'Sword' feature, is a remarkable challenge, climbed from the back of the cave, all the way along the razor edge...

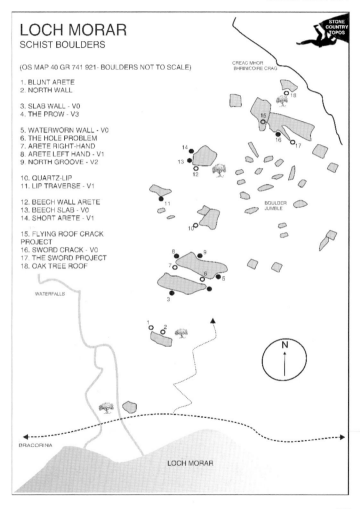

LOCH MORAR
SCHIST BOULDERS

(OS MAP 40 GR 741 921 - BOULDERS NOT TO SCALE)

1. BLUNT ARETE
2. NORTH WALL

3. SLAB WALL - V0
4. THE PROW - V3

5. WATERWORN WALL - V0
6. THE HOLE PROBLEM
7. ARETE RIGHT-HAND
8. ARETE LEFT HAND - V1
9. NORTH GROOVE - V2

10. QUARTZ-LIP
11. LIP TRAVERSE - V1

12. BEECH WALL ARETE
13. BEECH SLAB - V0
14. SHORT ARETE - V1

15. FLYING ROOF CRACK PROJECT
16. SWORD CRACK - V0
17. THE SWORD PROJECT
18. OAK TREE ROOF

CREAG MHOR BHRINICOIRE CRAG

BOULDER JUMBLE

WATERFALLS

N

BRACORINA

LOCH MORAR

TOUCHING SHARK SKIN ON SKYE

"The magic and magnetism (real and sentimental) of the great bare ridges of The Coolin grape blue in the morning sun..."

C. Douglas Milner – Rock for Climbing - 1950

Skye is a great geological museum of violent catastrophe and the slow tyranny of time and erosion. For the boulderer it has rock as varied as the sandstone of 'Kilta' (Portree) and Elgol; the dolerite jumble of Carn Liath (half way between Portree and Staffin); the Lewisian Gneiss of An Caol on Raasay and, of course, the wonderful gabbro of the great Coires such as Coire Lagan and Coire na Ghrunnda. Most of the recent bouldering has been developed by Si O'Conor and James Sutton, who have strapped boulder mats on to their adventurous backs and traipsed through the Coires, opening the ground for us to follow. Most of the great lines have been climbed on the big faces, but under their noses lie shapely lumps of fantastic climbing, none the worse for having left the mother-lode. Rock cares not a jot where it lays down its inherent movement. These stones of Skye are in no way diminished by the grandeur of their surroundings and if you can focus your mind on what climbing actually is, then the corrie floors are a mecca for wild bouldering jaunts. More than anywhere else in Scotland, this is the lair of legendary bouldering problems - wondrous beasts lost in the high amphitheatres of the Cuillin.

The Chieftain Arete, Coire Lagan.

"The Cuillin are an awesome revelation, where grandeur is obscured in mist and rainy visits, often condemned as an island of disappointment and dashed expectation. When it does dry out and clear after rain, the flanks of the cliffs gleam like rubbed armour, the sun beats like a heralding trumpet blast and great stones glitter on the corrie floors, maybe dwarfed by bigger scales, but invigorated by a sense of relative grandness. Their isolation is kingly, and if you doubt that, walk up from Glen Brittle and survey the boulders that have been deposited by a vanished glacier under the great lip of Coire Lagan. Their gabbro is like touching a shark that passes by in one awed moment."

James Sutton on 'The Thief's Arete', Coire Lagan,
and above, 'Pump Up the Jam, Coire na Ghrunnda.

GLEN BRITTLE
GABBRO BOULDERS

OS MAP 32 (BOULDERS NOT TO SCALE)

COIRE LAGAN COMPLEX

1. JAWBREAKER - V3
2. CRISS-CROSS - V4
3. NORTH-EAST ARETE - V5

4. HIGHBALL SLAB - V1
5. THE GROPER - V3
6. THE PINCH - V6
7. RIGHT ARETE - V4

8. THE RAMP - V1
9. THE FLUNKY - V2
10. LIFT ATTENDANT - V3
11. SKINS - V3

12. THE CHIEFTAIN - V4
13. LEFT ARETE - V5
14. THE GROOVE - V1
15. THE THIEF ARETE - V2

SRON NA CICHE COMPLEX

16. SNAKE ATTACK - V5
17. VENOM JAG - V11
18. BASS LINE VENOM - V4

19. HOWLING GAEL - V3
20. EVENING WINGS - V4
21. THUNDERHEAD - V7
22. MORNING WINGS - V5
23. IT'S OVER - V14

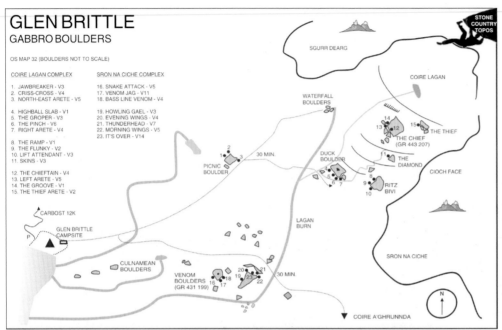

Clockwise:

1. Topping out on the Picnic Boulder
2. 'Morning Wings' on 'It's Over' Boulder
3. 'The Ramp', Ritz-Bivi
4. The Duck Boulder Arête
5. The classic 'Criss-Cross', Picnic Boulder

COIRE LAGAN BOULDERS

Having negotiated the Skye Bridge, the A87 winds through Broadford, on round Loch Ainort past the hump of Glamaig, then diminishes westwards at the Sligachan hotel onto the A863. After a few miles there is a left turn signed to Carbost, from where a minor road drops down through Glen Brittle. It is hard to keep your eyes on the road as the mighty mother-lode of the Cuillin looms. This is about where signals on mobiles simply vanish, compasses begin to quiver and even GPS begins to spit out a guess. The Culmeanan boulders lie along the south edge of the first stream, about ten minutes south of the campsite along the land rover track, offering nearby problems and traverses. To get to the main bouldering fields, follow the cobbled path up behind the WC block over the first false summit and up by the stream. A junction in the path is reached: left goes to Coire Lagan and right to the Sron na Ciche boulders. Usually a choice between how bold you are feeling or how strong...

On the north side of the Coire Lagan path, about thirty minutes from the campsite, and past the loch on the left, is the ledged block of 'The Picnic Boulder'. *Jawbreaker* climbs the crack on the west face. *Criss Cross* climbs the overhanging arête over the bog (do your duty and bring a stone from the path to help fill it in), clamping the seamed arête with toes and hands to stop swinging off into the pool. The *North East Arête* is Niall McNair's technical addition to this boulder, pretty much relying on feet smears all the way. The *East Face Crack* is a lot easier and climbs the vanishing crack to finish on slopers.

Continuing on a bit, the path forks up across two wee streams towards the Cioch buttress, where the main Coire Lagan boulders cluster, 'grape blue' and culled from the great faces of the Cioch. The 'Stream Boulder' has some good warm-up problems and is the first boulder in the Coire Lagan complex. The 'Duck Boulder' has two big stones perched on it. *The Duck Face* climbs the organically-veined rock on the left of this gravel-aproned boulder.

The *Right Arête* is a stretch to get started, but good holds gain height and a slap for the sloping bulge to the right allows the trucking slab to be gained. *The Pinch* is a couple of metres left of the right arête. Difficult pinching leads to a good left sidepull on the lip, then the right hand snaps to another lip pinch, from here it is a matter of willpower to fight through the small edges onto the slab. Just to the left again is *The Groper*. Jump to the bra-shaped hold and match a sloping hold above, then finish lengthily on better holds.

The 'Ritz Bivi' has three cracks above its entrance, all worthy of a tip. *The Flunky* climbs the excellent north crack and arête; *The Lift Attendant* bridges up over the bivi-wall and contorts into the diagonal crack. The right crack is also good and *The Ramp* (on the north-west face) looks easy, doesn't it? Another level up is the 'Diamond Boulder', on a small alp before the gathering of stones around 'The Chief'. The dark north side has a good sit-down project but requires a lot of spare skin to hold the lip. Right of the patina-edged west wall is *Skins*, which cranks from crimps right to the diagonal undercling to then follow the crack.

About another 100 metres higher up the Coire, 'The Chief' holds court over his clan of minor chieftains just below the Coire Lagan slabs. *The Chieftain* is a terrifying act of commitment up the scooped weakness of the west wall and the *Left Arête* is a slightly harder and even scarier teeter up the right side of the arête. More reasonable is *The Groove* which rocks up with increasing commitment to easier ground at the top.

Above The Chief is a line of scree. *The Thief* block lies above this. The obvious mantle of the lip is yet to be completed, but stepping left out onto the arête provides a good problem, though composure is needed above the sudden drop.

Over on the Sgurr Dearg side of Coire Lagan lie high buttresses and boulder fields, containing the yet-to-be-revealed locations of Si O'Conor's 'Extradition' and 'Darken Down the Day'.

The 'Lift Attendant', Ritz Bivi.

SRON NA CICHE BOULDERS

The Sron na Ciche boulders provide a less stressful atmosphere, but a rough and rude challenge to the boulderer's strength. The path to these boulders veers off right across the stream from the Coire Lagan path, past a wee loch to the lower reaches of the Coire Lagan burn. Just before the burn, turn right across a small bog and over the first brow appears the complex of *It's Over*.

It's Over is the awesome green face on the largest boulder, climbed with the utmost belief from a poor edge and undercut, twisting up desperately towards the sloper and right to the arête pinnacle. A hold was broken, but Si O'Conor reclaimed his original line on poorer holds in 2004. *Morning Wings* follows the slopey traverse right along the lip to finish up the left arête of It's Over, and *Evening Wings* applies the same philosophy to the right arête. *Thunderhead* is another hard addition on the boulder opposite *It's Over*, starting on the triangular nose, dropping down to the lip and traversing left to hopefully pull through onto the slab. A few metres to the right of Evening Wings is a wee bulging roof. Here the excellent *Howling Gael* pulls over into a diagonal seam and smears up right to finish.

200 metres further west is the fern-barbed peak of the Venom Boulder. The obvious sloper traverse of the south face is *Bass Line Venom,* slapping from right to left to finish round onto the slabbed corner. *Venom Jag* climbs straight up from the left end of the traverse from a poor edge and rail, aiming right for small edges. *Snake Attack* climbs the steep west face along a snaking flake crack to the slab and is one of the most under-estimated problems in the boulderfields of Sron na Ciche.

Gabbro is a fine rock to climb on, superbly rough, allowing some element of security on the more highball problems, but be warned, a day's hard session will strip the skin and finger-tape: Vaseline, vinegar or any other old-wife's remedy is required if you want to pull on again the next day! The best arrangements seem to echo the thoughts of Douglas Milner on the efforts required to climb in Skye, "...one day sitting and thinking, one day on the ridge, and one day just sitting...'"

The rest is exploration and excitement, for the Coires hold innumerable challenges and virgin boulders. James Sutton confirmed this with a remote exploration of Coire na Ghrunnda and discovered one of the best jamming crack climbs of its type in *Pump Up the Jam*, a ten metre V5 pulling along a perfect crack in a huge roof, way beyond the range of walkie-talkies and mobiles, way beyond the documented world, right in the heart of gabbro country...

The Venom Boulder.

'SOUL INVENTORY'

'Scottish bouldering... staring at the rock intently before each ascent of a problem... small bright green lichen...wrecked fingertips, blood leaking into the stone & a growing heat on the back after each completed line & each ascent...these were the first words that came to mind. And there's that thing, the mind. People are often more mindful of their fingers being dug into an edge & holding it at all costs than the power & impetus that's pulling them to move on. Momentum asks us to drop stance, smear & flow upward across the emptiness, fluid & light, than to fight the natural way of things. Climbers fail so often when they try to dictate movement to the rock, rather than listen to the rock's own regime of demands on the ascencionist. Nothing slips into the soul of a day's bouldering than one move perfectly executed. It's almost more important than the completion of a problem.Experimentation with movement & embracing its idiosyncrasies & anomalies will lead an individual to successful new horizons far quicker than his aim to simply be stronger than anyone else. It's not about being locked into what the teachers tell you. It's about expression & adaptation, questioning the teaching & having the self-confidence to execute the move. In that zone, there's no top & there's nowhere to fall. There's only the moment of commitment to the move, an instinctive reaction to the situation & a solution.

Strong Scottish ethics silently police & protect the rock for future generations. Chipping is out & humility towards unclimbable lines is in, preferring as we do, not to shout & moan, but to leave well alone until such time as a suitable talent comes along. Littering of the mountain environment is no more a selfish act attached to those with a lack of self or environmental respect. Honesty is paramount, grade debates are parody roaming the scene looking for victims, & today's boulderers huddle in close at a table or fire in the bar, throwing their hands into crux shapes, laughing wildly late into the night at the day's best falls or ascents, nudging each other over lopsided grins & mud-stained knees, they are not hard to find with their strong scent of enthusiasm. Things couldn't be more upbeat or passionate. Bouldering is finding a new gear.

At 38 years young, I continue to line up projects for future years, but whatever your ability there must be acceptance that we all degenerate & recede from the summit of our ambitions. If you believe that success involves bagging the highest grades imaginable you are mistaken.

Successful boulderers are ones that measure each increment of their achievements on a personal level. From the easiest slab to the most demanding overhang, it's all relevant when you discard comparison to the achievements of others. As I'm aware of the downward slope from the summit, I've always climbed with this in mind, there's no fight, no need to escape the cage of one day attaining a grey hair or two.

Moreover, I hope I'll be pulling down hard on a Font 6a in my 70's, still at the personal edge of my best, as a youth as intemperate as I once was grins & shouts back 'crank harder old basta'! What could mean more as I wave him on; to retain the awe of what it has meant to spend this life in amongst the boulders & shattered mountains of the Highlands?

*"...In that zone, there's no top
& there's nowhere to fall.
There's only the moment of
commitment to the move..."*

This is the life blood & progression in the development of Scottish bouldering, to let in the new, to lay down the challenge while we can & step gracefully aside for the future. There are harder more futuristic problems to go in Scotland than 'Extradition' & there are monster boulders to be tamed above the snow-line of the Cuillin on the mighty Clach Ceann-Feadhna. The question is simply who & when, not if.

To this end, I believe the future of bouldering will be taken high into the mountains. This is where the problems of tomorrow are waiting. Silent, snow covered & precipitous stones, struck like ancient petrified armies, watch us raven-eyed & unstirring from great heights.

It has always seemed a logical & natural progression to take the art into the void, to blue-sky & cut the threads of acceptability, to give it altitude & push mystic. It refreshes the meaning of & lays down a newness of self accountability to such words as 'challenge', 'explore' & 'venture'. Away from overcrowded circuits, away from manufactured problems crammed into ten meters of roadside rock, there is a silence, a cold breeze making its way through mountain rye grass, an occasional clatter of loose stone as an ice form gives way, clear water to wash away the chalk-stained bloodied hands & a spirit a million times older than the chattering temporal mind.

'It's Over', Sron na Ciche boulders.

'Darken down the Day' - Coire Lagan

Above this silent glistening sea, when we're all done - when we stare down at the shreds of finger tape like war torn flags shivering in the air & look back at the line we fought so hard to be master of, when we push our shoes into the sack & pull its weight onto sore shoulders to descend from the snow-line - they enter our dreams at night, these darkening cathedrals of stone. They become nothing more than an empty altar, accepting of the grades we dress them with, but remaining naked to their own ways, stilled once again like a dormant swimming pool from which the swimmers have retired.

And in that morning I will wake, there'll be a soft tapping of rain on the tent, a familiar light will stream through the Coire & the cooker will protest with a roar as I kick it into life for that first brew. I'll idly watch the next wave of boulderers flock towards gullied scree & moraine, encompassed in their own bubble of excited inaudible chatter, & I'll check the missing skin on my fingers for signs of healing.

Maybe I will wonder up through the grasses to that big flat boulder through the sunlight & watch them flicker like brightly coloured prairie birds picking clean the teeth of some giant Neolithic beast. Maybe I'll trundle over to the bar at Talisker, grab a dram & while away a few hours by the fire....before heading home.

The dog still has the stone I gave him up on the Cuillin ridge, he carried it all the way down, every step of the 3000 feet it takes to his bed, & he dreamed it into his soul inventory. Now he will take the stone home.

I guess the dog & I are similar that way...'

Si O'Conor 2004

'Extradition', Coire Lagan

'...the foot goes to the smear automatically, I don't ask it to. The base of the rehearsed bloc starts spluttering like an old weed-covered generator restored for its first fire-up in years, but it fires up & latent dormancy is memory. Engrams fire, unseen chemicals streaming through the body, time slows, the feet come off & I land out of the air on the next edge, fingers groaning & creaking under the pressure, but pain is an absent entity. Looking high for the next mark I feel my feet swing in, the weight & momentum of my legs as they course back to stone. They stick, my fingers breath out & like a wave retreating from a beach, my body weight draws out for the next quarter, to where the eye has already tasked the mind to be. There is control pilot, no deceleration, there is only this force & momentum, a subconscious reaction to stay with it.... I'm below my own arm pushing up into the edge, waiting for my weight to come away, waiting for the rush of cold shadowed air, for the painless white flash & pitched ringing, that receives a body fallen violently to earth...'

Si O'Conor - 'Extradition' thoughts

DUNTELCHAIG

Loch Duntelchaig lies on a heather moor above Inverness, its southern flanks littered with crags and boulders. Until recently the bouldering has been inexplicably ignored, for the crags have birthed some huge boulders and challenging lines jump out everywhere. The rock is a mossy gneiss, but where clean provides generous pulling on sharp incuts and small edges. Some obvious lines have been climbed in the pleasant 'main area' under the cracked orange crag, but many boulders lie hidden in the boulder fields beneath the crags, and exposed on the hillsides above, waiting for the boulderer's homecoming. The best time to visit is an autumn afternoon, or in a sunny spring, for the midges are bad here and the rock 'sweats' in the heat anyway. During a dry spell in winter, it is might be possible to claim some of the harder lines on the smoother holds.

If traveling along the A9 from the south, take the Daviot exit, a few miles before Inverness, and follow the single-track B851 road west over a bridge and towards Inverarnie. Once in the wee village turn right just after the football fields (the B861 to Inverness), and after a kilometer, take a left at a small crossroads. Follow this for a few miles to the crossroads at Dunlichity and go straight on. The road skirts a small loch and then arrives at the layby by the east end of Loch Duntelchaig. The Loch Duntelchaig crags and boulders are easily accessible from the loch-side path. Walk over the small dam and follow the path round for ten minutes past some huge boulder-fields (mostly too cluttered to provide good landings), take a left over a wee stream, unclip your mat and start bouldering.

Iain MacDonald - 'The Butterfly Collector', Duntelchaig area.

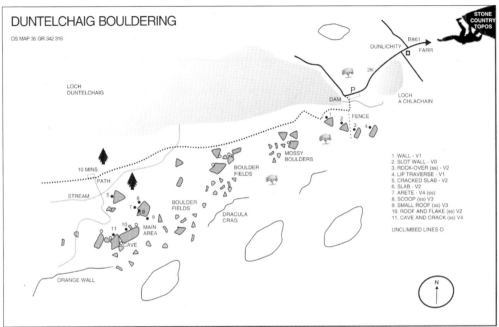

DUNTELCHAIG BOULDERING

OS MAP 35 GR 342 316

LOCH DUNTELCHAIG

LOCH A CHLACHAIN

DAM

DUNLICHITY

FARR

B861

STONE COUNTRY TOPOS

2K

P

FENCE

10 MINS.

PATH

STREAM

MOSSY BOULDERS

BOULDER FIELDS

BOULDER FIELDS

DRACULA CRAG

MAIN AREA

CAVE

ORANGE WALL

1. WALL - V1
2. SLOT WALL - V0
3. ROCK-OVER (ss) - V2
4. LIP TRAVERSE - V1
5. CRACKED SLAB - V2
6. SLAB - V2
7. ARETE - V4 (ss)
8. SCOOP (ss) V3
9. SMALL ROOF (ss) V3
10. ROOF AND FLAKE (ss) V2
11. CAVE AND CRACK (ss) V4

UNCLIMBED LINES O

N

Clockwise:

1. Iain Macdonald on the 'Outer Circuit'
2. Bouldering in the Main Area
3. On the endless Gneiss boulders...

'The Big Lobowski' traverse

'The Ruthven boulder, or the 'Bunnet Stane', is the Hulk of Scottish boulders, swollen with primeval stone anger, isolated and alone; bursting with gneiss veins; a steroid-pumped glacial erratic. It sat in the belly of a glacier metamorphosing, its underbelly becoming smoothed and bicep-ed, its upper surface roughened and abraded into mutant skin. Then it burst from its icy cocoon and howled its loneliness on a perfectly green tuft amongst the heather, until boulderers came along and gave it sympathy. Trevor Woods, our guide for the day, and its main developer and keeper, turned up on his bike from Inverness and showed us the tricks of this massive beast. It is so big, we were assured, that it is beyond the ability of all modern cranes to move. Perched above Loch Ruthven, it will not be budged by us: it sits there, fat-bellied and brooding with power and baseness. The bouldering requires commitment and grit and the moves are sweet and delicate despite the brutality of the approach required. Like the Hulk gently melting back into the human, the problems have a tender nature to them, with technique and knowledge and hard-earned familiarity their own rewards. It is not a kind boulder, nor is it gentle on your hands, but it is perfect, a sort of mutant-perfect - a lost creature: warped, muscular and transfixing.'

'Nefertiti'

THE RUTHVEN BOULDER

The boulder itself is easy to find. It sits quite visibly on a grassy knoll overlooking Loch Ruthven, south of Inverness. The B851 should be taken south-westwards from Daviot, through Farr to a right turn before East Croachy. The road crosses the River Nairn and winds down to a car-park beside Loch Ruthven, from where it is a short walk up through the heather to the stone.

The problems are described clockwise from the bulbous nose of *Barry Manilow*. This tremendous problem starts under the east roof and climbs up and right to holds beside the jugs, then reaches left to the bulbous nose where a desperate crawling mantel might gain a quartz hold just out of reach. To the left is an obvious flat sloping ledge. *Sloping Off* climbs from two small edges to gain the sloper, then a crux move right gains the ramp and a top-out rightwards. Going direct from the sloper up over the bulge is slightly easier.

The left arête is *Razor's Edge* which sit-starts at good edges and reaches for blind razors and continues up on crimps to a flake and direct finish. The groove round the corner is the excellent *Austin Powers*. Left of this is a wall beside the descent groove. The right side of this has a sloping ledge out of reach, which is gained from small edges, leading to a round hold and delicate finish, to give *The Cheeky Girls*.

Round the corner the west side has a roofed right arête opposite the 'baby bunnet' stone. *Rock'n' Roll Baby* starts on low jugs and traverses left to the crack until a rock-over can gain the slab. Left again is a wall. *Neil Armstrong* climbs from a horizontal crack directly up on quartz holds. The undercut arête facing the loch is *Shreddies*; a line can be climbed to the right of this - *The Big Tease* takes big quartz holds up and right.

The front face of the boulder holds some of the best problems on the stone: *The Big Lobowski* is a traverse along the low sloping rail; from the lowest incuts travel right to gain a sidepull and pull up on sharp holds leftwards to a crescent crimp, then aim for a small hold over the bulge to finish. *Outstanding* is the obvious line up and left from the start of the traverse incuts. Good incuts lead to a long throw for a quartz hold, then a long move to a jug allows a finish up and left on crystals. *Get Into the Groove* is the obvious challenge to the left again. A variation wanders left and up the wall at V4. The left-hand wall of the front face gives *Nefertiti* - start at two tiny edges and pop for the good hold, then move up right to an incut, from where a twisting reach up left gains a good edge, finishing by a layaway flake.

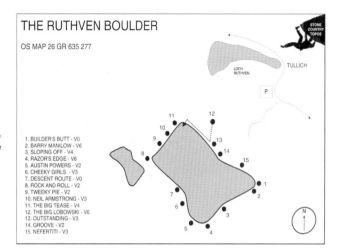

THE RUTHVEN BOULDER
OS MAP 26 GR 635 277

1. BUILDER'S BUTT - V0
2. BARRY MANILOW - V6
3. SLOPING OFF - V4
4. RAZOR'S EDGE - V6
5. AUSTIN POWERS - V2
6. CHEEKY GIRLS - V3
7. DESCENT ROUTE - V0
8. ROCK AND ROLL - V2
9. TWEEKY PIE - V2
10. NEIL ARMSTRONG - V3
11. THE BIG TEASE - V4
12. THE BIG LOBOWSKI - V6
13. OUTSTANDING - V6
14. GROOVE - V2
15. NEFERTITI - V3

Trev Woods on 'Barry Manilow'

109

Tim Rankin on the Turtle Traverse.

OF SEA PIGS AND SEA TURTLES

"Portlethen is a faded north-eastern fishing village just south of Aberdeen, blurred by the haar that seeps in off the North Sea and bleached by sunny rain-shadow days when the west is cursed with south-westerlies. The residents' gardens are decked with the dead memorabilia of the sea and everything feels like the detritus of time. It is easy to sit here and soak up the sun on a good day, listening to the seagulls squabble, feeling the boulder mat warm in the heat. You can wait for the Turtle boulder to rise bubbling out of the tide to dry its flanks. The shoreline itself is littered with scratched fishing floats, cloudy glass and plastic bottles and sleeping boulders. The schist boulders, squat and rubbed by the sea, have delightful textures, like chocolate sweets rubbed down to the hard toffee underneath. They suggest shapes to the mind, like clouds which have solidified and dropped to the ground. The Sea Turtle sits in a rock-pool and its tidal belly is veined and smooth as a turtle's shell, whereas the Sea Pig is a snouty little gem you feel floated in with the jetsam one day. Portlethen is a sea-salt's exotic collection of rock animals with strange and contorted features."

Adrian Crofton ably spotted on the Lost Wall, Portlethen.

PORTLETHEN
SCHIST BOULDERS

OS MAP 38 GR 934 959 (BOULDERS NOT TO SCALE)

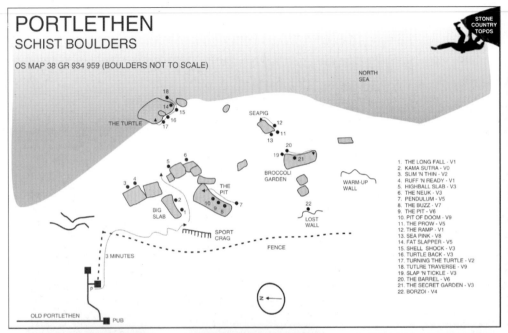

NORTH SEA

THE TURTLE

SEAPIG

BROCCOLI GARDEN

WARM-UP WALL

BIG SLAB

THE PIT

LOST WALL

SPORT CRAG

3 MINUTES

FENCE

OLD PORTLETHEN   PUB

1. THE LONG FALL · V1
2. KAMA SUTRA · V0
3. SLIM 'N THIN · V2
4. RUFF 'N READY · V1
5. HIGHBALL SLAB · V3
6. THE NEUK · V3
7. PENDULUM · V5
8. THE BUZZ · V7
9. THE PIT · V6
10. PIT OF DOOM · V9
11. THE PROW · V5
12. THE RAMP · V1
13. SEA PINK · V8
14. FAT SLAPPER · V5
15. SHELL SHOCK · V3
16. TURTLE BACK · V3
17. TURNING THE TURTLE · V2
18. TUTLRE TRAVERSE · V9
19. SLAP 'N TICKLE · V3
20. THE BARREL · V6
21. THE SECRET GARDEN · V3
22. BORZOI · V4

Clockwise;

1. Tim Rankin on 'Pendulum'
2. ...and on 'The Pit' Right-hand
3. On the slabs...
4. The 'Seapig ProwDirect'
5. Guy Robertson 'Ruff 'n Ready'

PORTLETHEN BOULDERING

Portlethen, or 'Old Portlethen', is situated midway between Stonehaven and Aberdeen off the A90. At the motorway flyover for Portlethen, make your way into the main village, then at a roundabout turn off over the railway bridge and follow a country road down to the old village, where careful parking must be found. The last cul de sac on the right has a small access path between the houses which swings left down past a pig field and right over a fence by the cliff-top. A bit further on there is access to the shore, where the boulders lie under a small sports crag.

On the approach down to the shore a gully leads past slabs to the shore. 'The Big Slab' on the left under the sports crag provides two excellent problems: *The Long Fall* with tricky climbing up the vague scoop to the top of the slab, and *Kama Sutra* which climbs to the apex of the slab straight up the middle.

'The Cube' is the slabby boulder down left of the above. The left edge can be climbed on its right side to give *Ruff and Ready* and the central line is a problem to focus the mind: *Slim and Thin*. Next to this is a mossy slab and then the 'Highball Slab' which hangs over a prop boulder. Pulling on to the right edge and climbing it gives the heart-flutterring *High Ball*. To the left is a small steep face. *The Neuk* is an excellent power problem climbing up through the face from a jammed boulder to a curious finish.

Once on the shore, clamber round right and up to a mezzanine to fight amongst the jetsam of the 'Pit Boulder'. The classic traverse of the lip is *Pendulum*: step off the left-hand spike and monkey rightwards along the lip, drop into the notch and crank out the right-hand groove. *The Buzz* climbs out of the pit from an undercut flake under the left roof: smear and pull hard to climb out left and up. For the classic tick: *The Pit* shares the same start but undercuts right and then straight up.

Another hard problem works out of the roof rightwards from 'The Pit', then undercuts to a notch via a thin crack to finish up 'Pendulum' to give *Pit of Doom*.

On the shore more achievable ambitions lie on the likes of 'The Sea Pig', the wee red-nosed boulder near the tidal line. *The Prow* - from a sitting start at the pocket climb the prow to its top, short but devious. Harder variations eliminate hands and feet - talk to Tim Rankin. *The Ramp* climbs the obvious seaward ramp from the jug right of the Prow pocket. *Sea Pink* climbs the thin crack left of the Prow, from a sit start of course.

Down left and well in the tidal rock pools, is the beautifully water-worn squat boulder of 'The Turtle'. The seaward-facing *Fat Slapper* sit starts at the lip sloper with feet on the jammed stone, then aims left to a good hold and rock-over. *Shell Shock* climbs up from the jug on the rock-pool arête, trending left to rock over. *Turtle Back* climbs up the shore side from the big jammed block, rightwards to slopers in a small corner, then up the left edge of the hanging arête. *Turning the Turtle* starts up Turtle Back to the lip jug and straight up. The classic though is the Turtle *Traverse*. From the slopers of 'Fat Slapper', traverse left around the lip under the arête on super rock and continue to finish up 'Turning the Turtle'.

The big lichen-covered boulder south of the rest is 'The Broccoli Garden'. Fortunately it has a clean underbelly. *Slap and Tickle* sit starts under the north arête and launches up this to rock over onto the slab. *The Barrel* starts sitting on the north wall and traverses left staying under the lip to finish up the left edge. *The Secret Garden* sit starts at a break, cranks for a sidepull on the lip and over.

'The Lost Wall' provides a wee gem in *Borzoi*, which climbs from the corner rightwards to gain the arête and slab. Plenty of smaller boulders and walls provide the rest of the entertainment and complement the zoo of movement that is Portlethen.

Clockwise:
1. The Luath Prow
2. Rowie Beaton on the Mouse boulder
3. Stuart Stronach on 'Slim Shady'

THE LUATH STONES

High on the hill above Alford in Aberdeenshire, can be seen a large prow of rock keeping sentinel over the Don valley. Surrounding this large post of rock, to which Cuchulainn may have tied his hound, are numerous schist boulders providing playful bouldering problems and a fine area to picnic in the summer. They were developed by Stuart Stronach and Jo MacLeod in 2002 and now provide a pleasant diversion for the itinerant boulderer. The boulders can easily be walked up to through dirt tracks from the back of the walled house in the forested estate – parking can be found behind this. The entrance to the estate is via a gatehouse after the village of Whitehouse, just before the junction of the A944 and B992, a few kilometres east of the town of Alford.

The bouldering has good flat landings, is never too highball and the smaller oddly-shaped boulders such as The 'Sherman Tank' boulder provide quality traverses and friction problems. *The Boar-Hound's Leash* is a superb traverse along the steeper lip of this boulder from left to right to finish up the right arête and *Cuchulainn* climbs the left side of the wee prow from a sitting start. The excellent *Traverse Link* climbs from the left arête all the way around the slab and prow to finish along The Boar Hound's Leash.

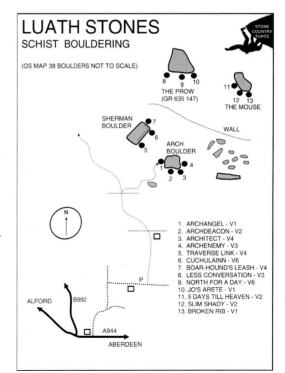

The Arch boulder is the first significant boulder encountered, with a tiger-striped main arched face. *Archbishop* bridges up the obvious left scoop finishing right at the arête. *Archangel* takes the arête on its right side, *Archdeacon* takes the flake in the central wall and *Architect* is the difficult right arête from a sitting start. *Archenemy* is the puzzling arête slab on the east face, and can be climbed statically with technique and faith.

'The Prow' itself has a desperate test-piece in the central problem of *North for a Day*, which is a tip-bursting excursion up the tiger-striped face from the seam, traveling slightly right, then back into the high scoop to finish direct. The right arête on the left side is *Jo's Arête* and the left arête is the excellent sloper exercise of *A Little Less Conversation*.

'The Mouse' is the offwidth-split hump of rock to the right of The Prow. The best problem is *Five Days Till Heaven* which climbs the hanging crack just right of the main offwidth. *Slim Shady* takes the groove on the far right of the wall. *Broken Rib* takes the arête at the far south end of the west face with a high and exciting crux. The rest of the boulders can be played on and traversed at will and many imaginative combinations and sitting starts add to the relaxed bouldering atmosphere.

LUATH STONES
SCHIST BOULDERING

(OS MAP 38 BOULDERS NOT TO SCALE)

THE PROW (GR 635 147)

THE MOUSE

SHERMAN BOULDER

WALL

ARCH BOULDER

ALFORD — B992

A944 — ABERDEEN

1. ARCHANGEL - V1
2. ARCHDEACON - V2
3. ARCHITECT - V4
4. ARCHENEMY - V3
5. TRAVERSE LINK - V4
6. CUCHULAINN - V6
7. BOAR-HOUND'S LEASH - V4
8. LESS CONVERSATION - V3
9. NORTH FOR A DAY - V6
10. JO'S ARETE - V1
11. 5 DAYS TILL HEAVEN - V2
12. SLIM SHADY - V2
13. BROKEN RIB - V1

115

'The Jerker', Cummingston

NORTHERN LIGHTS

"The Moray Coast is a fine place to see the Aurora Borealis, listen to jet fighters squealing through the skies, or simply boulder. From the granite caves of Cullen to the sandstone of Cummingston, the weather here is cool and kind with only the occasional haar to dampen the holds. Cummingston itself is the best place on this coast to boulder, offering fierce finger-testpieces or butch pocket-pulling on a hard orange sandstone of the Triassic era, not as old and hard as the Torridonian stuff, but superb nonetheless, brushing down to a chalky patina not unlike the egdes and slopers of Fontainebleau. On the vertical problems, steel fingers are essential and new shoes, not your old blunted pair, with good pointy edges to dig into those small nicks, make some problems feasible rather than impossible. On the steeper problems, it is all a matter of hard shoulder-pulling on slopers and pockets, brushing them down with a toothbrush to a clean, cool texture, but don't linger too long and in the heat or they turn into soap bars. The caves provide good bouldering on a warm summer's day, as their sandy textures dry and harden, and the crimpy walls are a test of technique and subtle body-posture. This is a venue where your bouldering mat will take a pounding if your technique is out of shape."

CUMMINGSTON
PERMIAN SANDSTONE

(OS MAP 28 - GR 130 692)

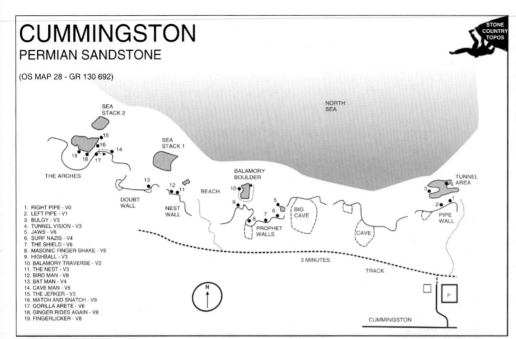

SEA STACK 2

NORTH SEA

15
16
14
19 18 17

THE ARCHES

SEA STACK 1

BALAMORY BOULDER

10

DOUBT WALL

13

12 11

BEACH

NEST WALL

9
8
7 6 5
BIG CAVE

PROPHET WALLS

CAVE

TUNNEL AREA
4
3
2 1
PIPE WALL

1. RIGHT PIPE - V0
2. LEFT PIPE - V1
3. BULGY - V3
4. TUNNEL VISION - V3
5. JAWS - V6
6. SURF NAZIS - V4
7. THE SHIELD - V6
8. MASONIC FINGER-SHAKE - V6
9. HIGHBALL - V3
10. BALAMORY TRAVERSE - V2
11. THE NEST - V3
12. BIRD MAN - V8
13. BAT MAN - V4
14. CAVE MAN - V5
15. THE JERKER - V3
16. MATCH AND SNATCH - V9
17. GORILLA ARETE - V6
18. GINGER RIDES AGAIN - V8
19. FINGERLICKER - V8

3 MINUTES

TRACK

N

CUMMINGSTON

P

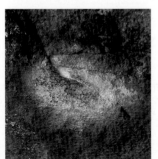

Clockwise:

1. Iain MacDonald on 'Match & Snatch'
2. Charlie Hornsby on 'Cave Man'
3. Iain MacDonald on 'Gorilla Arete'
4. Dougie Wheeler ' Ring of Bright Water'
5. Cummingston hold

STONE COUNTRY TOPOS

CUMMINGSTON BOULDERING

Situated between Lossiemouth and Burghead on the B9040 north of Elgin, the crags and associated bouldering are easily found once in the linear village of Cummingston. Take a seawards turn into Seaview Road, just east of a white memorial cross, turn left, then right and park beside the play park. The Tunnel area is straight below the car park, whereas the Seastack areas are a short walk westwards along the old railway cutting. The crags have been bouldered on for years, mainly by Nick Clements, but the bouldering has only recently been fully developed, mainly by Iain MacDonald and friends. Most of the bouldering is on the crags and finished at climb-downs, or jump-offs, but on most problems, reaching these will feel like a just accomplishment.

The 'Tunnel Area' is a good place to warm up. The Pipe Wall, split by an eponymous iron drainage pipe, has some good bold warm-up problems. *The Flake*, three metres right of the pipe, leads to good finishing holds, and *Pipe Wall*, just left of the pipe, is a little stretchier at the top after the break. The Tunnel itself provides some good problems, though the holds may be a bit sandy after absorbing the haar. *Tunnel Vision* starts on the north wall bulge in the cave and traverses right along the obvious break to a jug undercut which gains the central roof-flake, then lock up to a pocketed wall and rock over to finish. On the south wall of the cave, *Bulgy* climbs the west end of the cave from a sit start at pockets. Crimp and pocket up to a jug, then climb a chicken-headed wall with a long reach right to finish.

The 'Prophet Area', opposite the sea stacks, provides good bouldering. From east to west the best problems are: *Jaws* - the small boulder at the east end of the crags has a short prow, three moves long, from a sit start on pinches. On the crag to the west of this is *Surf Nazis*, which climbs the wall below the peg, cranking up on underclings to a ferned slot, gain another undercling, reach jugs and jump off. *The Shield* climbs the obvious shield of rock round the corner to the right - from holds on the left slap desperately rightwards, aiming for crimps up and right, then stand on the wee ledge to finish. Just right again, on the other side of the cave is the puzzling *Masonic Finger-shake*, which takes the mono with the left hand and climbs to a thin break. *Highball* takes the slopered wall right of the first corner opposite the Balamory boulder, climbing up and right to escape.

On the fine 'Balamory Boulder', the best problem is the full *Traverse*, starting on the descent ramp, then climb anti-clockwise round the boulder to finish up the seaward east arête.

Further west, just before the sea stacks, is 'Nest Wall'. The obvious *Nest* climbs the awkward square-cut corner to the jump-off jug at 'the nest' ledge. *Bird Man* is a hard problem from the thin crack on the left, gaining the slot, then traversing thinly up and right to the nest. 'Doubt Wall' is the shingle-washed wall opposite the big sea stack. *Bat Man* climbs out of the wee cave on the left, pulling up on pinches to the left wall to finish at a jug up and right.

The 'Cave Area', opposite the next sea stack eastwards, is a fine spot. The big bulging wall with the obvious horizontal break provides the superb and reversible *Cave Man*. From the left arête, pull up to the lower line of pockets and monkey rightwards to midway jugs, then drop down to edges and stretch to the right arête to finish, or reverse until you drop. The right arête from a sit-start is *Gorilla*.

The front face of the cave has the classic bulging arête of *The Jerker*. Just opposite the stack, climb the prow from holds on the left and pull up and round the arête to finishing jugs. Inside the cave, the north wall has the excellent *Fingerlicker*. This climbs from the 'gap' up and right to a finishing jug, along a complex sequence of punishing holds. One of the hardest problems at Cummingston is *Match and Snatch*. This starts on a rib just left of The Jerker, then traverses left round into the cave to reverse Fingerlicker to finish at an apt crucifix position at 'the gap'. The bulging arête between these last two problems can be climbed heel-hooking out from the crack to a hard sequence on slopers up to finishing jugs on the arête, to give *Ginger Rides Again*.

119

A frequent posture on 'Wide-Eyed', Craigmore.

BOULDERING AND FAILURE

"The words of the great writer Samuel Beckett – 'Fail again, fail better...' – might actually be the mantra for the modern boulderer. The whole process of bouldering has more to do with how you cope with failure than how you enjoy success. Success can be enjoyed for what it is without much thinking (usually with a whoop and a Lou Ferrino pose), but failing on a problem you have tried dozens, if not hundreds of times, poses a real mental stopper in how you deal with this failure... What am I doing wrong? Am I too weak? Is this the wrong sequence? Are conditions right? Maybe I'm not cut out for this? Is there a hold I'm missing? These and other questions whittle away at your bouldering resolve all the time, making the goal of success both distant and hallowed at the same time, sometimes turning a bouldering session into a sit-on-the-mat-and stare-into-space day.

These are the low points. Truly the measure of the best boulderers is humility, an ability to accept these doubts and hear them, but not to give into them by throwing your shoes in the ocean and selling your boulder mat... an understanding of failure is the best we can do as humans and bouldering is no different. You have to take the increments as success. These are the tricks – turn one move into a goal for the day. Hang that sloping hold, shift your centre of gravity, try digging in a thumb pinch... suddenly you're hanging where you fell last time. You jump off, excited by such a small and seemingly insignificant improvement. You are still nowhere near completing the problem, but something has opened inside you – visualization suddenly flows like an internal movie and mentally you can see the rest unfolding. You chalk up in a hurry, you rehearse that tiny success, over and over. You go home tired, flappers hanging off un-hardened skin, beaten up, tendons aching, needing three day's rest, having carted your mats into this lonely glen for hours just to hang off that one hold again.

This is the boulderer failing better... these are the tiny zen tricks of the art and they can only be learnt by failing again and again, without getting all humpty about it...until one day success comes, and it's not the big deal you thought it was, in fact it's not really the point at all - you almost wish you were back at that point weeks ago, where that single twist of the hip, that thumb-sprag, that hidden toe-hook, released the failure for a moment... gave you that golden glimpse, sharpened your eye, made you love this game again."

APPLECROSS
TORRIDONIAN SANDSTONE

(OS MAP 24 - BOULDERS NOT TO SCALE)

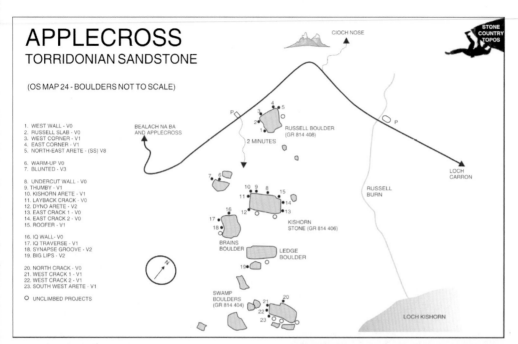

CIOCH NOSE

BEALACH NA BA AND APPLECROSS

2 MINUTES

RUSSELL BOULDER (GR 814 408)

LOCH CARRON

RUSSELL BURN

KISHORN STONE (GR 814 406)

BRAINS BOULDER

LEDGE BOULDER

SWAMP BOULDERS (GR 814 404)

LOCH KISHORN

STONE COUNTRY TOPOS

1. WEST WALL - V0
2. RUSSELL SLAB - V0
3. WEST CORNER - V1
4. EAST CORNER - V1
5. NORTH-EAST ARETE - (SS) V8

6. WARM-UP - V0
7. BLUNTED - V3

8. UNDERCUT WALL - V0
9. THUMBY - V1
10. KISHORN ARETE - V1
11. LAYBACK CRACK - V0
12. DYNO ARETE - V2
13. EAST CRACK 1 - V0
14. EAST CRACK 2 - V0
15. ROOFER - V1

16. IQ WALL - V0
17. IQ TRAVERSE - V1
18. SYNAPSE GROOVE - V2
19. BIG LIPS - V2

20. NORTH CRACK - V0
21. WEST CRACK 1 - V1
22. WEST CRACK 2 - V1
23. SOUTH WEST ARETE - V1

O UNCLIMBED PROJECTS

"Travelling to the North West of Scotland fills any climber with hyperactivity, much like a spoilt child with Giant Smarties, there are just too many boulders to swallow in one go and things get a bit manic. It is best to pick an area, stay there a while and get used to the balanced tension of climbing on Torridonian sandstone, learning the angles of the sloping holds, what pebbles can be stood on, what apparent jugs you gamble on hitting with a dynamic throw... as good an area to learn these tricks of nuance and experience would be the great boulders looking out over Loch Kishorn under the nose of Sgurr a' Chaorachain."

'Brains boulder'

Applecross sandstone

APPLECROSS BOULDERING

Dumped by a long-vanished glacier, these stones were plucked from Coire nan Arr and deposited on a blunt ridge west of the Russell Burn. They are only minutes from the ever-steepening Bealach na Ba road to Applecross, a few miles west of Lochcarron, and best approached from a small layby one kilometer after the bridge over the Russell burn. The largest is the obvious Kishorn boulder, which distracts the eye as you climb the road. Most of the climbing is in the easier grades and the rock is clean and heavily featured, the landings are good and there are plenty of new projects and open lines still to be climbed on the boulders.

Approaching from the road, the 'Kishorn Boulder' is the main point of reference. Its delightful north face has many good introductory wall lines, with the northwest arête providing a suitable exercise in balance. The undercling problem just to the left also provides a moment of essential control. The south face is steeper and blanker with some obvious project challenges such as the hanging groove which is frustratingly just out of reach. The east face has two good easy cracks and the west face a fine northwest layback crack.

Just down below and to the west is the 'Brains Boulder', which is so well textured and featured you wish you could airlift it to your back garden. Its west face has a good travelling crack started from the arête and the east face groove provides a technical bridging exercise, with a choice of exiting left or right.

Downhill again is the large 'Ledge Boulder', which has a heavily ledged south face, which is problematic in that it is slightly green and highball and crevassed enough to be terrifying. The wee boulder below it has a more amenable juggy traverse on a roof.

Further downhill again are the 'Swamp Boulders'. The best of these is the east boulder. Its west wall has two good cracks, its east wall has a propped roof problem, but the south wall has the best problems here. The main projectclimbs the wall and groove right of the west arête, cranking up to a good finger hold, then posing a tricky conundrum as to how to gain the small flake edges up and right. The bulging roof to the right can be monkeyed up on good slopers but is not as generous for the feet.

Higher up near the road and overlooking the burn is the 'Russell Boulder'. It has a highball slabby west face, a double-cornered north face and a steep and powerful project on the east face. The north-east arête is an excellent blunt power problem on diminishing slopers from a sit-down start. The project wall remains - a desperate underclinging exercise to small finger slopers.

Applecross

TORRIDON
'THE CELTIC JUMBLE'

OS MAP 24 - GR 998 507 (BOULDERS NOT TO SCALE)

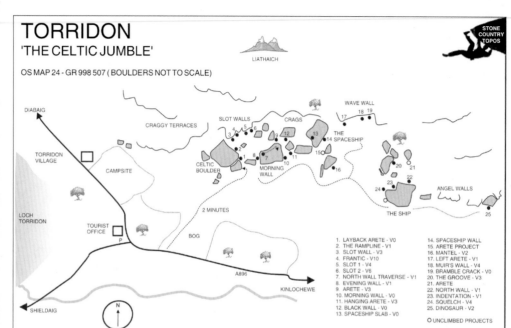

LIATHAICH

STONE COUNTRY TOPOS

DIABAIG

CRAGGY TERRACES

TORRIDON VILLAGE

CAMPSITE

LOCH TORRIDON

TOURIST OFFICE

P

2 MINUTES

BOG

A896

KINLOCHEWE

SHIELDAIG

N

SLOT WALLS

CRAGS

WAVE WALL

CELTIC BOULDER

MORNING WALL

THE SPACESHIP

THE SHIP

ANGEL WALLS

1. LAYBACK ARETE - V0
2. THE RAMPLINE - V1
3. SLOT WALL - V3
4. FRANTIC - V10
5. SLOT 1 - V4
6. SLOT 2 - V6
7. NORTH WALL TRAVERSE - V1
8. EVENING WALL - V1
9. ARETE - V3
10. MORNING WALL - V0
11. HANGING ARETE - V3
12. BLACK WALL - V0
13. SPACESHIP SLAB - V0

14. SPACESHIP WALL
15. ARETE PROJECT
16. MANTEL - V2
17. LEFT ARETE - V1
18. MUIR'S WALL - V4
19. BRAMBLE CRACK - V0
20. THE GROOVE - V3
21. ARETE
22. NORTH WALL - V1
23. INDENTATION - V1
24. SQUELCH - V4
25. DINOSAUR - V2

○ UNCLIMBED PROJECTS

THE CELTIC JUMBLE OF TORRIDON

"Coming down the single-track A896 road into Torridon, past the giant of Liathach on the right and the red terraces of Torridonian sandstone on the left, you might be forgiven for suffering from a conscience of scale. As a boulderer, do not be put off by the obvious grandeur, but pitch your tent in the wee campsite by the village, then go exploring the crags and boulders that cleave and lean from the terraced hillsides all the way up to the high ridges. It would be impossible to exhaust the climbing in this area, or document every delightful Pre-Cambrian boulder, so we will make do with a small tour of the 'Celtic Jumble' of rocks just east of the campsite."

Lef to right:

1. 'Tiptoe Wall'
2. Celtic Carving
3. 'Squelch', the Ship Boulder

124

TORRIDON

From the Tourist Information centre, walk back up the A896 a hundred yards, then cross the bog between the two plantations in a north-east direction. The first boulder lies under a leaning crag and if you look round its back side, you will find the carved slab of the 'Celtic Boulder'. *The Rampline* climbs left to right over the symbol and the more direct slab line to the right of the symbol is *Scott's Wall*. *The Layback Arête* on the east face is the descent route, climbing up the ramp and arête over the plinth of rock. If you're feeling brave, a step across the boulder to the crag wall gives an alternative if worrying exit.

Across from this boulder the crag leans steeply. *Slot Wall* climbs the right side of the first leaning wall from a sitting start. Gain the slot, then a good ledge, cross over to a high hold by the heather and finish up the high easy slab. Left of the big arête is the desperate sloper problem *Frantic*. From undercuts gain the lip slopers and traverse left to pull over at the crack. Right of the big arête is another leaning wall. *Slot 1* gains the left hand slot from a sitting start and cranks out to easier ground. *Slot 2* is a harder proposition, with the sit start crux to the right-hand slot leading to a crimp and slopers to pull over the lip.

'Morning Wall' has a fine east face with good easy lines and a good traverse on its north side. Just to the right of this boulder is the obvious *Hanging Arête* - from good holds at the lip, heel-hook and press up to better holds and an easier top-out. Further right still, the 'Spaceship Boulder' has some good easy padding slabs and a bulging unclimbed east face.

The 'Mantle Boulder' lies down and right of the Spaceship, over the edge of the bog. *The Mantle* climbs the centre of the wall via the midway ledge and using the blank groove to cleverly press up to slopers and top-out.

A short walk east leads to a collection of boulders round the obvious giant that is the 'Ship Boulder'. The 'Tree Boulder' has a good east face *Groove* just left of the cave above a black pool.

'The Ship' itself suffers from squeezing up bilge-water with its own weight, but if you have a mat and can place flat stones

strategically, the problems are worthwhile. *Squelch* is the obvious challenge of the west hanging arête, butching up footless to a difficult top-out on slopers, hence the name! *Indentation* is the groove just left of Squelch, finishing left of the prow. *The North Wall* is a high and exciting wall problem, with just enough holds to avoid too much insecurity at the top. The rippled south wall still remains to be climbed.

Up and left above the Ship boulders is 'Wave Wall'. The *Left Arête* is highball and *Bramble Crack* is the easier right hand crack. Just left of this is the direct line of *Muir's Wall*. A short walk to the right of the Ship is a low overhanging red crag, known as The Angel. Good traverses can be had here and a hard cave sit start pulls through the roof on the left. Furthest right is the distinctive club-foot of The Dinosaur. The blunt arête of this prehistoric 'foot' is a tricky problem pulling into the break, the crack to the right is V0 and a good traverse can be made left along the crack. Plenty more projects remain here in this accessible and enjoyable jumble of suggestive boulders.

'Fight Club', the Trossachs.

Andy Gallagher - Scottish bouldering guru

Colin Lampton on 'The Main Issue' at Reiff-in-the-Woods

A PRECAMBRIAN DARKNESS

"North of Ullapool, the landscape ages dramatically: cores of Precambrian Torridonian sandstone have been gnawed down by the invisible teeth of time to produce the great peaks and buttresses of Coigach. Turning west off the A835 down towards Achiltibuie and Reiff, the single-track road winds along Loch Lurgainn under Cul Beag to the unmistakeable towers of Stac Pollaidh. Two kilometres after the car-park to this remarkable peak, just before the road drops down to Loch Bad a' Ghaill, the forested hill overlooking a craggy peninsula hides some of the best of the extensive bouldering in Coigach. A small parking layby lies at the top of the hill and the boulders and walls can be explored at will over generally mossy landings. The pebbled red sandstone is hard and baked, rasps against the fingers and provides the feet with remarkable friction. Most problems, due to the generous sculpture of the rock, lie in the V0-V3 category, with some hard steeper lines providing the impetus for future return. Being so accessible, yet so hidden, and in such a wild landscape, this arcadia of bouldering exhibits the generosity of superb climbing and constant movement for which Coigach is rightly renowned."

'REIFF IN THE WOODS'
TORRIDONIAN SANDSTONE BOULDERS

OS MAP 15 - GR 091 094

STONE COUNTRY TOPOS

STAC POLLAIDH

REIFF AND ACHILTIBUIE

ULLAPOOL

P

2K

P

PICNIC PLINTH

N

LOCH BAD A'GHAILL

DESCENT

SOLO WALLS

CRAG

CRAG

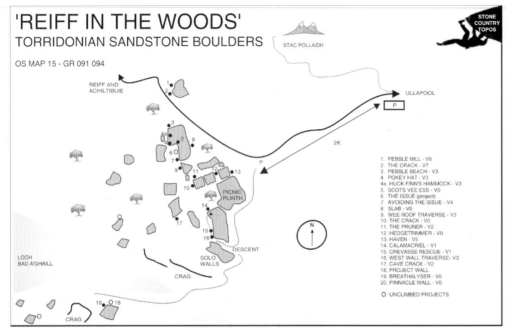

1. PEBBLE MILL - V6
2. THE CRACK - V7
3. PEBBLE BEACH - V3
4. POKEY HAT - V3
4a. HUCK FINN'S HAMMOCK - V3
5. SCOTS VEE ESS - V0
6. THE ISSUE (project)
7. AVOIDING THE ISSUE - V4
8. SLAB - V0
9. WEE ROOF TRAVERSE - V3
10. THE CRACK - V0
11. THE PRUNER - V2
12. HEDGETRIMMER - V0
13. HAVEN - V5
14. CALAMACRIEL - V1
15. CREVASSE RESCUE - V1
16. WEST WALL TRAVERSE - V3
17. CAVE CRACK - V2
18. PROJECT WALL
19. BREATHALYSER - V0
20. PINNACLE WALL - V0

O UNCLIMBED PROJECTS

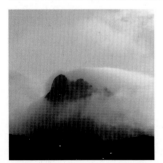

Clockwise:

1. West Wall Traverse
2. Torridonian Pebbles
3. Reuben on the Cubes
4. Technique is all you need
5. Stac Pollaidh view

'REIFF IN THE WOODS' BOULDERING

The boulder on the north side of the road, hidden in some trees, provides two sweet problems, both spotted by Mike Tweedley on his flashing raids north. *Pebble Mill* is a hard problem illustrating the faith in one small pebble's attachment to its mother-lode. Heel-hooking and hard pulling on the blunt arête allows the pebble to be gained and eventually the high crack. *The Crack* is the obvious and deceptive challenge of the crack. It looks endowed with good sidepulls and it is, but starting down low on the right and traversing up and left leads to a desperate lunge for the holds high in the crack. Flailing feet want to push off something that just isn't there.

Across the road in the wooded area is the jungle of main boulders, developed as a main bouldering venue by Ian Taylor and friends. *Pebble Beach* is a delightful problem. From a standing start on the left of the arête, it is trickier than it looks to get your feet on the big sloping ledge, then it is even harder to find a sequence to gain the top. Balance and faith are the keys. The overhanging side of the arête is a different matter. *Pokey Hat* is a similar act of commitment to the last problem. It is easy enough to get to half height, but the final layaway at the apex of the arête is frustratingly hard to reach and the landing feels scary, though nothing an attentive spotter can't relieve. Traversing left along the overhanging rail above the trees gives *Huck Finn's Hammock*, an excellent if ankle-worrying jug-haul. *Scots Vee Ess* climbs the very traditional Scottish corner, employing more thrutch than elegance. *The Main Issue* is the challenge of the severely overhanging wall with its half-height railing. A twisting stretch and body tension gains the railing and a short traverse right to better holds leads to the quandary of whether to dyno for the blank lip, or stretch right to a beckoning crack… *Avoiding the Issue* takes the sloping ramp on the right from a sitting start, slapping left to reach awkwardly up to the back of the ramp. On the back of this boulder, facing the road, are some enjoyable short slab climbs.

Wee Roof Traverse is an excellent little number traversing right on slopers to gain a crack and mantle. It is a lot easier with clever technique. 'The Cubes' provide some vertical wall climbing at all grades. *The Crack* is a fine little climb which can be finished direct or wander left up a flake crack on superb holds. The arête to the left of this is an enjoyable shoulder–tightener. Round the corner is *The Pruner* which climbs the dark wall on small edges. *Hedgetrimmer* is the obvious dank crack in the pit and the cube nearest the road has a fine blank wall which is climbed on the left to give *Haven*, with the arête unable to be used at first. A jump gains small sidepulls and height is gained by a difficult press move to a flake with the right hand and smearing contortionism allows the arête to be used to finish the problem.

Underneath the picnic plinth is a deep amphitheatre surrounded by walls, just down from the cubes. *Calamacriel* climbs the blankest part of the chock-stoned north wall near the arête. Good positioning of the feet allows a final flat ledge to be gained but it is a stretch and the toes often plop off the small slopers. Round the corner is the excellently featured overhanging scoop of the west wall, which catches fire in the evening light. The superb *West Wall Traverse* starts at the descent gully and stays low most of the way, with the crux reaching the horizontal crack and final sloping ledges near the arête. Various straight-up problems can be done on excellent holds, such as the juggy *Crevasse Rescue* on the right side of the wall.

Down another level is the Howff boulder. *Cave Crack* is a tricky and fingery stretch out over the bottomless arête by the Howff. Below this are more hidden boulders and pinnacles, with some good easy high problems and fine slabs.

Across the Loch there is a huge boulder under the towered crag. It is a well-maintained howff with an elegant interior patio and its undercut west wall has a fine running rail which gives *Breathalyser*. Some seriously hard problems lurk on this boulder and its potential is still to be unleashed.

BLOODSTONES

"In the far northwest of Scotland, where the roads suddenly narrow to single lane without warning, and shops close randomly, the landscape is unknowingly old - a rolling glaciated core of Lewisian gneiss, its veins injected with the volcanic stimulants of red granite and black basalt. Every blunt ridge has a line of erratic stones like toy animals placed there by a playful geology. The land is mostly stone and water, the glaciers have long vanished and vegetation lays a thin shredded veil of green and brown where it can. For the boulderer it is a paradise of exploration. Scattered on the whispering grasses and spongy bogs lie hundreds of stones, the small hills are flanked by steep craglets and clean slabs of gneiss, in the dips and hollows lie some huge boulders. The whole area is by its nature an open book, mocking our attempts to document its stone through its secretive and remote scale."

Clockwise:

1. 'Blood Music'
2. The 'Bloodstone'
3. Laxford geology

RHICONICH BOULDERING

A good example of the bouldering here, and easily accessible, are the large boulders north of the one-horse town of Rhiconich, where the road winds its lonesome way to Durness through a barren landscape but for the stones. About two kilometers north of the Rhiconich hotel, the road summits at a craggy hill, and just to the east of the road is the obvious granite-bellied 'Blood Stone'. Surrounded by small bouldering crags and other boulders, it provides the meat of the climbing, its west facing red-stained overhang in particular.

The obvious high crack of *Odysseus* is endowed with excellent holds at first, but these run out as the rock drops away beneath and the crack becomes flared and the feet struggle to find purchase. The Gods are invoked at the top-out. Just to the right of the crack is the superb red wall of *Blood Music*. This mighty problem starts sitting in the obvious red cave, throws up to excellent holds and large pockets, then launches out right to a crux sequence through now smaller, broken holds. Just right of the red wall is the bottomless prow of *Penelope*, which climbs from a crimp and layaway to good holds at half-height, then it is a long stretch to the lip and a difficult high sequence onto the slab. The *Cyclops Arête* can be gained from the large grey south-facing wall and its juggy groove climbed on the left side. The Traveller boulder has some enjoyable easy crack climbs and the North boulders provide a collection of good problems and projects, especially on the Flake boulder, with the cleanest rock on the south faces.

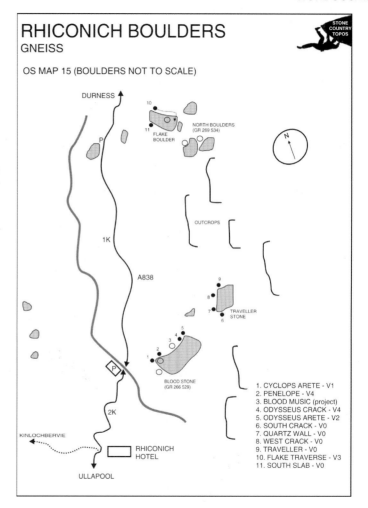

RHICONICH BOULDERS
GNEISS

OS MAP 15 (BOULDERS NOT TO SCALE)

DURNESS

NORTH BOULDERS
(GR 269 534)

FLAKE BOULDER

OUTCROPS

1K

A838

TRAVELLER STONE

BLOOD STONE
(GR 266 529)

2K

KINLOCHBERVIE

RHICONICH HOTEL

ULLAPOOL

1. CYCLOPS ARETE - V1
2. PENELOPE - V4
3. BLOOD MUSIC (project)
4. ODYSSEUS CRACK - V4
5. ODYSSEUS ARETE - V2
6. SOUTH CRACK - V0
7. QUARTZ WALL - V0
8. WEST CRACK - V0
9. TRAVELLER - V0
10. FLAKE TRAVERSE - V3
11. SOUTH SLAB - V0

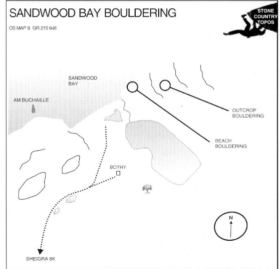

SANDWOOD BAY BOULDERING

OS MAP 9   GR 215 648

STONE
COUNTRY
TOPOS

SANDWOOD
BAY

AM BUCHAILLE

OUTCROP
BOULDERING

BEACH
BOULDERING

BOTHY

N

SHEIGRA 8K

SANDWOOD BAY

Historically an excellent far north-west bouldering area. The weather-worn gneiss walls at Sandwood Bay, on the lonely walk to Cape Wrath, have been bouldered on for decades by visiting climbers. They can be approached by a walk north from Sheigra, where the B801 from Rhiconich passes through Kinlochbervie and ends suddenly. From the campsite at Sheigra it is an 8km walk, so it's a long day out for bouldering unless you're prepared to bothy at Strathcallaidh or camp at Sandwood itself. A good idea would be to combine this with good weather on the beach, or along with a plan to climb the Am Buchaille sea-stack. The bouldering is on superb gneiss, bitten down to a rough texture by the ceaseless Atlantic forces. The bouldering on the northern beaches is excellent but indescribable, as the level of the sand can change things dramatically. On the northern headlands lean some excellent steep walls with traverses and straight-ups... there is plenty of scope for the top-end raider, though most of the obvious lines have been sniffed out by visiting parties over the years, so it is not a place to worry about first ascents - they don't seem to matter at such a venue! By the time you get there, all thoughts of colonisation will be lost to the winds and the humbling scale of elements - one of the best venues in Scotland to learn the art of disappearing.

"...this place is about being, so grades are even less relevent here..."

Dave Wheeler

Left: Dave Wheeler on Sandwood Gneiss (Pizza Wall)
Above:Rob Hampton on the Eastern traverse (Pizza Wall)
Opposite: Dave Wheeler on the beach

Clockwise:

1. The Semaphore Stack - Aird beach
2. 'HyperBallad' - Eoropaidh
3. 'Deltics' - The Boneyard
4. 'Early distant warning' - Sea Peanut - Port Nis

THE BUTT OF LEWIS

Lewis is a boggy wilderness with a hard under storey of Lewisian Gneiss which outcrops round the coastal fringes like a geological enclosure. The cliffs are solid and sea hardened, boulders are regularly flung up by giant waves and the whole land can suffer the full brunt of nature. The best of the bouldering is around the Butt of Lewis. Port Nis beach has eroded sea boulders and coves (GR 538 634), west is Eoropaidh (Hyper Ballad area GR 510 651) and the Bone-Yard (GR 507 641) and at the Aird beach at Dhail (Dell) is the secluded Semaphore Stacks area (GR 466 611). The climbing is distributed in hidden coves, on sudden beaches and headlands. It is home to some very hard problems, but the scope is at all grades and a summer holiday could easily be lost to nothing but new bouldering. More details can be found on www.scottishclimbs.com, or on www.skye-bloc.blog.ac

At Port Nis, along the beach from the harbour, are some tidal walls and boulders. *Synchronicity* is an excellent traverse of the big hanging prow along the obvious break to finish up and past the prow. On the next leaning wall, three ledges provide the campus-board problem of *1-5-9*. Ten metres beyond is the awesome roof of *Trace Element of Life*, cranking desperately from the ledge down left and into the hanging finger-tip crack to pull through the roof. *Hydrophobic* is a good inland traverse on the second of the three eroded boulders to finish up the steep arête. *Pea-Butt Nutter* is the seaward side of the washed-up 'Sea Peanut', following the rising slopey lip. On the other side of the boulder, the lipped roof is followed left to a blunt arête to give *Early Distant Warning*.

Eoropaidh is a village on the road to Port Nis, on west coast towards the Butt of Lewis. From the west end of the village climb a gate and walk straight across a field to find a secluded cove. Here lie two throat-gulping problems next to each other on a steep roof. *Hyper Ballad* starts at low slopers on the blunt arête to a series of edges off right, then more slopers through the steep wall onto the headwall to a highball finish. *Grip Crisis (Griem Eiginn)* shares the same start but goes left along tiny crimps to match the lip and fight through the headwall by the leaning block.

'The Bone Yard 'area lies south of the big strand and dune system, west of the old cemetery. From the village, gain the beach, walk to its end and round a wee headland is 'The Bone-Yard'. *Coral* climbs the white cave from a boss undercut along crimps to finish on the flat arête. *Qualified* climbs the deep cave on sharp crimps out onto a painful finish up the headwall. *Deltics* sit starts at the back wall, then goes through the roof at its widest section onto the big rail, then a thin finish above this.

Further south is the village of Dell (Dhail), from where a lovely wee beach can be found – the Aird - southwest of the village along tracks by the lochans, west of Knockan Dibadale. The tallest stack provides the excellent problem of *Semaphores*, from the steep nose butch through poor slopers, go left and climb the central face into cracked groove. *Hemispheres* goes right from the same start and takes the blank wall on small crimps to a large crack. *Walk an extra Mile* is the good traverse on the impending cliff behind the Semaphore stack, starting in the recess and out to the steep corner to finish at the obvious gully on the far left. *Epitaxy* takes the gob smacking leaning arête, claiming the best natural line on the Aird beach.

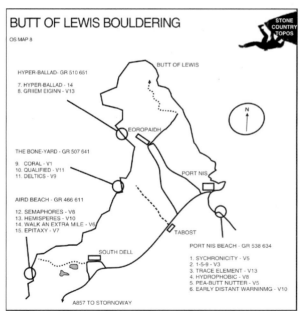

BUTT OF LEWIS BOULDERING

OS MAP 8

STONE COUNTRY TOPOS

BUTT OF LEWIS

HYPER-BALLAD- GR 510 651
7. HYPER-BALLAD - 14
8. GRIIEM EIGINN - V13

EOROPAIDH

THE BONE-YARD - GR 507 641
9. CORAL - V1
10. QUALIFIED - V11
11. DELTICS - V9

PORT NIS

AIRD BEACH - GR 466 611
12. SEMAPHORES - V8
13. HEMISPERES - V10
14. WALK AN EXTRA MILE - V6
15. EPITAXY - V7

TABOST

SOUTH DELL

PORT NIS BEACH - GR 538 634
1. SYCHRONICITI - V5
2. 1-5-9 - V3
3. TRACE ELEMENT - V13
4. HYDROPHOBIC - V8
5. PEA-BUTT NUTTER - V5
6. EARLY DISTANT WARNINMG - V10

A857 TO STORNOWAY

OTHER AREAS

ARDMAIR - ULLAPOOL (OS Map 15 GR 108 980)
Developed by Ian Taylor and local Ullapool climbers, this sea-eroded belly of sandstone lies at the Rhue end of Ardmair beach, just over the hill from Ullapool. The bouldering lies over the pebble beach and provides short butch sloper-pulling and long lippy traverses. Across the road is the 'Ardmair Ruins' area, developed by Mike Tweedley. About 80 metres along the wee crags lies a propped block with the hard problem of 'Crucifix' V8/9, climbing out from the small boulder on undercuts to finish up the corner. More details can be found on www.scottishclimbs.com

ANNAT - TORRIDON (OS Map 24 GR 899 545)
An area of much potential, these boulders lie above the wee village of Annat just southwest of Torridon on the A896. They can be approached by parking at the graveyard and walking up through the trees on the left. Dave MacLeod and Mike Tweedley found a classic in 'Three Streaks' V7 – a sit-start groove on a small streaked wall 10 metres left of an obvious Cube boulder. The rock is reported to be excellent and further problems are likely to fall. See www.scottishclimbs.com

ISLE OF RUM (OS Map 39)
 Possibly the most unique are the incredibly clean and rough 'allivalite' boulders perched on heather under the east flank of Hallival in Coire nan Gruund (GR 397 958). They can be approached by climbing Hallival and dropping down, or by the pleasant path from Kinloch to veer off up the Allt na h'Uamh burn up into the corrie.

MULL – FIONNPHORT (OS Map 48 GR 302 232)
Apart from the excellent gabbro at Loch Buie, Fionnphort - on the west tip of the Ross of Mull - has some excellent pink granite walls for endless exploration. It is a place to explore at will and without fuss of documentation. There is an excellent campsite at Fidden. There is also potential on the island of Erraid. See www.scottishclimbs.com

SHETLAND – STANES OF STOFAST (OS Map 2 GR 505 720)
Shetland is our most remote climbing outlier and home to some ancient stones. The huge Gneiss boulders called the 'Stanes of Stofast' have recently been developed by Paul and Al Whitworth. They lie north of Lerwick on the remote Lunna Ness peninsula. Passing through Vidlin, the small road finally ends at Outrabister, from where the stones are on the hillside south-east. More details can be found on www.climbshetland.co.uk

Left to right from top:

1. Fionnphort granite
2. 'Little Cracker' - Stofast
3. '3 Streaks', Annat
4. 'Buddhafinger', Glen Massan
5. Stanes of Stofast

SKYE – CARN LIATH (OS Map 23 GR 494 563)
Aside from the great (and painful!) gabbro boulders of Coire Lagan, there is also a collection of finer-grained basalt boulders at Carn Liath off the A855 to Staffin. About 13km north of Portree, before the hamlet of Rigg and the conifer plantations, two burns tumble down from Carn Liath hill on the west. Approach up the main grassy ridge and skirt round the steep hill in a northwesterly direction to find the main boulderfield after about 40 minutes. It is a place to explore at will, though a good guide is available from James Sutton (this can be bought at the Glen Brittle campsite shop), who developed the area and rates it as the most satisfying bouldering in Skye.

Left to right from top:

1. 'Virgin Suicides' - Stronachlachlar
2. 'Babylon' - Adam's Rock
3. 'Red Craigs' - Glen Clova
4. 'Bladerunner' - Glen Massan
5. 'My Evil Twin' - Sandyhills

ABERDEENSHIRE - ADAM'S ROCK (OS Map 38 GR 630 192)
Northwest of Aberdeen, on the A944, turn right onto the B992 at Whitehouse, then follow this to a T-junction at Keig, turn right then right again shortly after and follow a B-road east for 2k. Park in a layby on the right just before fields. Follow the forestry track, then take a track leading off right uphill. Take a left fork to the boulder itself. Plenty of amenable bouldering on clean granite, with the classic being 'Babylon' V4, which slaps up the right side of the obvious arête. Please be discreet, as raptors nest nearby!

GLEN CLOVA – CAIRNGORMS (OS Map 44)
For Dundee climbers, this is probably the most local area for future development. There are boulders all along the glen and hidden in the forests, but the best would probably be along the north-east loop of the Glen Clova road north of Kirriemuir, and at the road-end, especially under the Red Craigs at GR 293 755.

CRANBERRY ROCKS - CAIRNGORMS (OS Map 36 GR 001 069)
If you're doing a course at Glenmore Lodge near Aviemore, this is a good local bouldering spot. Follow the road up to the Cairngorm ski-station car-park in Coire na Ciste and follow the chair-lift up to the granite boulders on the left (10 minutes). Lots of sloping granite problems in the V0-V3 range. Mike Gale has produced a guide for this and other Strathspey areas - enquire at Glenmore Lodge.

STRONACHLACHLAR – LOCH ARKLET (OS Map 56 GR 392 100)
Above Loch Arklet a fantastic hidden garden of bolted crags looks over some tumbled boulders. These are obvious and best approached from the T-junction at the turn right to Stronachlachlar in the Trossachs (10 km north of Aberfoyle on the B829). The best boulder is the long tall stone just under the old forest. Just behind this excellent boulder, a long stone gives the right-to-left lip traverse of Dave Redpath's 'Virgin Suicides' V6.

WOLFCRAG – STIRLING (OS Map GR 789 980)
An old sandstone quarry above Bridge of Allan west of Stirling, this provides some excellent bouldering and eliminates. The problems require careful description and have 'rules' - they are all well described in a topo on www.scottishclimbs.com

GLEN MASSAN – COWAL (OS Map 63 GR 117 866)
Excellent schist bouldering at the road-end in Glen Massan, north of Dunoon in Cowal. Discovered by Mike Tweedley, the best boulder is the huge 'House Boulder' behind Stonefield farm and this is home to the superb traverse of the front face left-to-right to give 'Bladerunner' V8. A topo is available at www.scottishclimbs.com

SANDY HILLS – DUMFRIES (OS Map 84 GR 891 547)
Another hard spot from Paul Savage! From Sandyhills bay on the A710, walk west along the beach and round the headland, where a weird prow can be found in a tidal cave. This is climbed without recourse to big holds nearby to give the desperate 'My Evil Twin', at a mighty grade of V12.

LENDALFOOT BEACH - AYRSHIRE (OS Map 76 GR 131 901)
An excellent beach bouldering venue, these boulders lie on the sandy beach at Lendalfoot, a few miles south of Girvan on the A77 to Stranraer. They have steep waterworn walls and roofs, usually best on the seaward sides at low-tide. There is a rumoured Paul Savage V11 on the main boulder...

'Crocodile', Glen Massan.

BOULDERING AND TIME

"Geology, with its time-lapse patience, stares us out as climbers. It does not reveal itself too obviously in our momentary time scales. Rock just looks a little too much like rock to be seen as anything else. However, to the boulderer, a boulder is more like a solid cloud, suggesting movement and time stirred together: its 'shape' is seen as its structure of movement, all dictated by the slow pressures of unimaginable time. Bouldering, in essence, re-imagines this time, gives form to it. Hence the excitement engendered by great stones on those who love to climb them: the thought of granite; of gabbro; of basalt; fills us with a kind of emotional, 'rocky' endearment. We can feel - scrambling, colourful rats that we are – the beautiful shape-legacy of geology, just as a skateboarder understands the sudden curves of asphalt, or a surfer the burgeoning wave: time opens up into pure movement and those long wastes of unconscious time are given a moment of vision from their darkness.

In the Mahayana tradition of Buddhism, there is a method of erasing the delusions of time called 'Skilful Means', which consists of spiritual shortcuts from the Dharma: sayings to frazzle the brain into a kind of temporary Nirvana. But might not bouldering also lead to this suspension of self-delusion? After all, why might enlightenment not be granted by a trick of physical movement: a toe-hook, or a thumb-sprag? A skilful means will erase the gravity of the boulder, and though this achievement may be as long as coming in an assault on an Alpine peak, we could not achieve our noisy, fist-pumping ecstasies without some secret methods, would we?"

Tim Morozzo bags 'Mugsy', Dumbarton Rock.

The Past and the Future

The future of Scottish bouldering will be the natural continuation of a climbing tradition. The same philosophy and approach is rigorously required by the landscape - the rock and stones themselves mould the activists into a hardened, holistic thing: maybe a shard of exfoliated bravado; or a gentle rounded thing of time and experience; or a brief blurred lens of howling motion.

There is a long thread of mystique and solitary drama about climbing in Scotland - personal heroics done without fuss in a primal amphitheatre. Bell inherited something of Collie, Murray of Bell, Nimlin of Murray, Cunningham of Nimlin, Robin Smith of Cunningham, Patey's deeds moved among the lonely cliffs like ball lightning... so when we inherited the inner fractals of bouldering, we carried the tradition into the stones... Gallagher developed the focus of Cuthbertson, Mal Smith looked deeper into seemingly impossible dreamtime.

Now a whole new crop of boulderers find an old tradition unfolding in these remote boulders. There is so much more to be found, and not just in a physical sense, away from the roads, in the high Corries, on the tips of stormy Island peninsulas: places where compasses spin, and mobiles die and forums mean nothing. At some point the borders dissolve and it is all adventure... you will walk your own ghost through histories, laying down another layer of why we climb in the first place.

'Mòr-Fhairge' - Skigersta, Lewis

Acknowledgements

This book owes its existence to the contribution and enthusiasm of the following: Sandra Spence, Tim Morozzo, Dave MacLeod, Colin Lampton, Kev Howett, Rory Howett, Mike Tweedley, Kirsty and Graham McBirnie, Pete Murray, Tim Carruthers, Trevor Woods (good scran!), Tim Rankin, Si O'Conor, James Sutton, Mal Meech, Ian Taylor, Steve Richardson, Adrian Crofton, Guy Robertson, Jo George, Dave Cuthbertson, Niall McNair, Dave Redpath, Stuart Stronach, Chris Graham, Dave Wheeler, Iain MacDonald, Gary Vincent... the list goes on... thanks to all those who went bouldering with us.

PHOTO CREDITS

All photos by:
Tim Morozzo (www.morozzo.co.uk) and John Watson (www.stonecountry.co.uk) except:

Kev Howett: Pages 56, 57, 58, 59 www.mountaineering-scotland.org.uk
Si O'Conor: Pages 102, 103, 104, 105, 136, 143 www.skyebloc.blog.ac
Dave Cuthbertson: Pages 68 (Pic1), 69 (Pic 1), 88 - www.cubbyimages.com
Dave MacLeod: Pages 42 (Pics 2, 3, 5), 44 (Pic 2), 138 (Pic 3), 139 (Pic 5)
Kevin Curry: Page 85
Stuart Stronach: Pages 114 (Pics 2,3) 139 (Pic 2)
Dave Redpath: Pages 43 (Pic 1), 69 (Pic 2), 139 (Pic 1)
Paul Savage: Pages 14 (Pic 3), 15 (Pic 1)
Mike Tweedley: Pages 16 (Pics 2, 3, 4), 44 (Pic 1), 138 (Pics 1, 4), 139 (Pic 4)
Paul Whitworth: Page 138 (Pics 2, 5) www.climbshetland.co.uk
David Wheeler: Pages 106, 118 (Pics 1-4), 134, 135

Also thanks to www.scottishclimbs.com for their dedication to the eternal 'now' of Scottish bouldering...